Laelius
Sive
de Amicitia
Dialogus

Other Cicero Titles
from Bolchazy-Carducci Publishers, Inc.

Cicero: Pro Archia Poeta Oratio, 2nd Ed.
Steven M. Cerutti
ISBN: 978-0-86516-642-4, student edition

Cicero: Pro Archia Poeta Oratio, Teacher's Guide
Linda Fabrizio
ISBN: 978-0-86516-616-5, teacher's guide

*Cicero: Pro Archia Poeta Oratio: A Structural Analysis
of the Speech and Companion to the Commentary*
Steven M. Cerutti
ISBN: 978-0-86516-439-0

Cicero's De Amicitia: AP* Selections
Sheila K. Dickison, Patsy Rodden Ricks
ISBN: 978-0-86516-639-4, student edition
ISBN: 978-0-86516-641-7, teacher's guide

A Cicero Workbook
Judy Hayes, Jane Crawford
ISBN: 978-0-86516-643-1, student edition
ISBN: 978-0-86516-654-7, teacher's manual

Cicero's First Catilinarian Oration
Karl Frerichs
ISBN: 978-0-86516-341-3

Cicero's Pro Caelio: AP* Edition, 3rd edition
Stephen Ciraolo
ISBN: 978-0-86516-559-5

Cicero: On Old Age/De Senectute
Charles E. Bennet
ISBN: 978-0-86516-001-5

*Completely Parsed Cicero
The First Oration of Cicero Against Catiline*
Archibald A. Maclardy
ISBN: 978-0-86516-590-8

Cicero The Patriot
Rose Williams
ISBN: 978-0-86516-587-8, student edition
ISBN: 978-0-86516-588-5, teacher's edition

Comedy in the Pro Caelio
Katherine A. Geffcken
ISBN: 978-0-86516-287-5

CICERO
de Amicitia

H. E. GOULD
AND
J. L. WHITELEY

Bolchazy-Carducci Publishers, Inc.
Wauconda, Illinois USA

Cover illustration
Cicero, a bust in the Capitoline Museum, Rome.

Cicero: de Amicitia

H. E. Gould and J. L. Whiteley

First published by MacMillan & Co. Ltd. 1941
Reprinted, with permission of MacMillan Education Ltd.

Bolchazy-Carducci Publishers, Inc.
1000 Brown Street
Wauconda, IL 60084 USA
www.bolchazy.com

Printed in the United States of America
2007
by United Graphics

ISBN 978-0-86516-042-2

CONTENTS

LIST OF ILLUSTRATIONS

FOREWORD

IN preparing this book the editors have followed the scheme which they outlined in the foreword to the first volume in this series, *Civil War in Spain*, viz. : a reliable text (in this case the text in the Macmillan Elementary Classics Series has been very carefully revised), suitable illustrations, a vocabulary that gives only those meanings that are required, and last and perhaps most important of all, adequate assistance in the Notes, so that the student may feel capable of translating with confidence and accuracy.

H. E. G.

BIDEFORD, 1941   J. L. W.

INTRODUCTION

(i) Marcus Tullius Cicero

Cicero was born near Arpinum on January 3rd, 106 B.C., and lost his life in December, 43 B.C., in the proscriptions which Antony organised in the troubled period which followed Caesar's murder. Cicero's life, then, covers the period which saw the collapse of the Roman Republic and the beginning of what was to be the Roman Principate in which the Emperors had the powers of dictators.

He began his career as a lawyer and had such brilliant success at the Roman bar that he was able, although not a member of the governing class, to obtain the regular sequence of magistracies and a seat in the senate. He spent his quaestorship in Sicily, where his conduct was marked by honesty and disinterestedness, and, finally in 51 B.C., he held a provincial governorship in Cilicia, south-east Asia Minor. Cicero's vanity and pride in the fact that he had climbed to the highest offices in the state by his own merit and ability, made him very attached to the constitutional forms of the Roman Republic, and blinded him to the many political and social evils

vii

of the day, such as the narrow-mindedness and selfishness of the ruling class, the senatorial order, its failure to provide a strong and efficient government either in Rome or in the provinces and, above all, its inability to control the successful generals and their armies who were destined to overthrow the Republic.

A short sketch of some of the most important issues at stake in the political sphere during this century will help to make Cicero's position clear.

Theoretically the Roman Republic was democratic in its working, but in reality all the power lay in the hands of a few families identified with the senate, whose ambition it was to retain the reins of government to the exclusion of all others. A generation before Cicero's birth, their political supremacy had been temporarily shaken by two ardent reformers, the Gracchi brothers, Tiberius and Gaius, who seem to have made an honest attempt to solve several serious problems, such as unemployment, the disappearance of the small farmer, and the relations between Rome and her allies in Italy. The senate put every obstacle in their path, and eventually the Gracchi [1] lost their lives in street fighting, and the senatorial order quickly re-established its supremacy.

[1] For more details, see the notes on Chap. xi. ll. 5, 6, 10, 48; Chap. xii. ll. 8-9, 10.

In the first century B.C., however, the senate had to
meet further attacks from other reformers, and, as
both sides were now resorting to force, they both
looked for support to the outstanding general of the
day who could get bills passed with the aid of his
troops. Thus civil war broke out and it was char-
acterised by cruelty and massacre on both sides.

For example, during the second decade of the first
century, when Cicero was just beginning his career
at the bar, there were three civil wars, and Rome
was twice besieged and captured by Roman generals
in command of Roman and Italian troops. More
horrible still, in 80 B.C. Sulla began the system of
'proscriptions', under which all those whose political
opinions were regarded as dangerous to the winning
side could be killed with impunity.

The next twenty years, 80–60 B.C., were momen-
tous in the history of the Roman Republic. Sulla's
attempt to bolster up the power of the senate gradually collapsed before attacks from several quarters,
especially from Pompey and Caesar, the latter of whom
was beginning to take an active part in politics.

During this period, Cicero had established his reputation as a lawyer and orator, and, in particular, he
had distinguished himself by a successful prosecution
of Verres for misgovernment in Sicily. At this time,
too, he entered political life, became aedile in 69,

praetor in 66, and consul in 63 B.C. His consular
year of office will always be remembered for the
vigorous way in which he crushed a dangerous
attempt to effect a *coup d'état* on the part of Catiline,
an unscrupulous noble who hoped to rally to his side
the many discontented elements in Italy. The fact
that there was so much discontent in Italy is a strong
indictment of the senatorial government of the preceding seventy years.

Cicero attempted to form a strong government,
capable of maintaining order in Rome and the provinces, and of controlling the recklessness of dema-
gogic tribunes and their irresponsible followers
among the landless and workless mob in Rome. He
aimed at establishing a kind of ' National Government ', a combination of senators, business men and
financiers, and of the upper classes in the Italian
cities, protected by a loyal general and a strong force
of troops. He cast Pompey for the rôle of protector
of the constitution.

Such an ideal, however, failed to work. In the
first place, in 60 B.C., the alliance between Caesar,
Pompey and Crassus, known as the First Triumvirate, showed that the senate had now lost all power
of independent action. Secondly, there was Julius
Caesar to be reckoned with, an ambitious man who
gradually came to realise that the Roman Republic

was too far gone for remedial treatment, and should be replaced by a new system.

Thus, during the next sixteen years, 60–44 B.C., Cicero's political ideal was completely shattered. He himself was exiled in 58 [1] and recalled in 57 B.C. During 58–51 B.C. Caesar was adding to the Roman province, a new and rich Empire, Gaul, which he annexed after a brilliant series of campaigns. In Rome itself constitutional government broke down and anarchy became so widespread that the senate had to call in Pompey and his troops to restore order. Gradually the senate succeeded in alienating Pompey from Caesar, and in 49 B.C. civil war broke out between Caesar and the senate, led by Pompey.

It took Caesar four years to crush the senatorial party, and by 45 B.C. he was virtually the sole ruler of the Roman Empire. A year later, he was assassinated by a group of senators led by Brutus, who seems to have honestly believed that with Caesar removed, the Roman Republic would be restored to its former position.

If we are to understand Cicero's feelings at this time, his distress at his exile, his unrestrained joy at his recall, his dismay at the dictatorial position of

---

[1] The reason for his exile was that during his consulship in 63 B.C., he had executed without trial certain fellow-conspirators of Catiline.

Julius Caesar, and his delight at his murder, we have to remember that to Cicero, a political career in what he considered a free state with democratic forms of government, was the only legitimate career for a free man. He could never forget that he himself had risen to the top and won the consulship and a seat in the senate by his own ability and merit. He failed to see, as Caesar saw clearly enough, that the Republic was past mending. Thus after Caesar's murder, Cicero attempted once more to form a ' National Government '. Not only did he fail once more, but he lost his own life. For he had embittered Antony, Caesar's successor, and, when the Second Triumvirate was formed, consisting of Antony, Lepidus and Octavian, Antony got his revenge by having Cicero's name put down on the list of the proscribed.

(ii) THE WORKS OF CICERO

The works of Cicero may be divided into three groups : (i) his speeches, both legal and political, by which he established an undisputed reputation as the master of Roman eloquence ; (ii) his voluminous correspondence which gives us a picture of Roman political and social life under the later republic, more vivid and varied than that of any other period of Roman history ; and finally (iii) his philosophical works, in which he aimed at explaining and criticising for the benefit of educated Romans, the doctrines and tenets of the leading Greek philosophical schools. Under (iii) we may classify the two essays on ' Old Age ' and ' Friendship '.

In the latter, which is the subject of this edition, Cicero imitates the practice of the Greek philosophers, by putting his essay in the form of a dialogue, only, of course, with Roman characters. Such a practice gives more dramatic interest to the work and enables the author to introduce names and allusions to historical events.

To help students to follow the reasoning more easily, an analysis of the argument is placed at the head of each chapter.

A Coin of Cornuficius,
friend and correspondent
of Cicero.

Left : A Figure repre-
senting the Emperor
Augustus as Augur.

Both illustrations show clearly the wand or *lituus,* which was used
for marking out the heavens for augury. Cf. the note on Chap. I, l. 1.

M. TULLI CICERONIS

LAELIUS SIVE DE AMICITIA DIALOGUS

CHAPTER I

Dedication to Atticus.

1. Q. Mucius augur multa narrare de C. Laelio
socero suo memoriter et iucunde solebat nec dubitare
illum in omni sermone appellare sapientem. Ego
autem a patre ita eram deductus ad Scaevolam
sumpta virili toga, ut, quoad possem et liceret, a 5
senis latere nunquam discederem. Itaque multa ab
eo prudenter disputata, multa etiam breviter et
commode dicta memoriae mandabam, fierique stud-
ebam eius prudentia doctior. Quo mortuo me ad
pontificem Scaevolam contuli, quem unum nostrae 10
civitatis et ingenio et iustitia praestantissimum audeo
dicere. Sed de hoc alias : nunc redeo ad augurem.

2. Cum saepe multa, tum memini domi in
hemicyclio sedentem, ut solebat, cum et ego essem
una et pauci admodum familiares, in eum sermonem 15
illum incidere qui tum fere multis erat in ore.
Meministi enim profecto, Attice, et eo magis quod
P. Sulpicio utebare multum, cum is tribunus plebis
capitali odio a Q. Pompeio, qui tum erat consul,

20 dissideret, quocum coniunctissime et amantissime
vixerat, quanta esset hominum vel admiratio vel
querella. 3. Itaque tum Scaevola, cum in eam ipsam
mentionem incidisset, exposuit nobis sermonem
Laeli de amicitia habitum ab illo secum et cum
25 altero genero C. Fannio, M. F. paucis diebus post
mortem Africani. Eius disputationis sententias
memoriae mandavi, quas hoc libro exposui arbitratu
meo ; quasi enim ipsos induxi loquentes, ne ' inquam ' et ' inquit ' saepius interponeretur atque ut
30 tamquam a praesentibus coram haberi sermo videretur. Cum enim saepe mecum ageres ut de
amicitia scriberem aliquid, digna mihi res cum
omnium cognitione tum nostra familiaritate visa est.
Itaque feci non invitus ut prodessem multis rogatu
35 tuo. 4. Sed ut in Catone Maiore, qui est scriptus
ad te de senectute, Catonem induxi senem disputan-
tem, quia nulla videbatur aptior persona quae de illa
aetate loqueretur, quam eius qui et diutissime senex
fuisset et in ipsa senectute praeter ceteros floruisset ;
40 sic, cum accepissemus a patribus maxime memora-
bilem C. Laeli et P. Scipionis familiaritatem fuisse,
idonea mihi Laeli persona visa est quae de amicitia
ea ipsa dissereret quae disputata ab eo meminisset
Scaevola. Genus autem hoc sermonum positum in
45 hominum veterum auctoritate et eorum illustrium
plus nescio quo pacto videtur habere gravitatis.

Itaque ipse mea legens sic adficior interdum ut Catonem, non me, loqui existimem. 5. Sed ut tum ad senem senex de senectute, sic hoc libro ad amicum amicissimus de amicitia scripsi. Tum est 50 Cato locutus quo erat nemo fere senior temporibus illis, nemo prudentior : nunc Laelius et sapiens, sic enim est habitus, et amicitiae gloria excellens de amicitia loquetur. Tu velim animum a me parumper avertas, Laelium loqui ipsum putes. C. Fannius 55 et Q. Mucius ad socerum veniunt post mortem Africani : ab his sermo oritur, respondet Laelius, cuius tota disputatio est de amicitia, quam legens tu te ipse cognosces.

CHAPTER II

FANNIUS : *Many men have been given the title ' Sapiens ',* *Laelius, but you deserve it for your devotion to learning* *as well as for your character. Many too are anxious to* *know how you bear the death of your friend Scipio.*

LAELIUS : *I thank you for the compliment, but Cato surely was* *Sapiens if any one was for the way he bore his son's death.*

6. FANNIUS. Sunt ista, Laeli, nec enim melior vir fuit Africano quisquam nec clarior. Sed existimare debes omnium oculos nunc in te esse coniectos; unum te sapientem et appellant et existimant. Tribuebatur hoc modo M. Catoni ; scimus L. 5 Atilium apud patres nostros appellatum esse sapientem : sed uterque alio quodam modo ; Atilius quia

prudens esse in iure civili putabatur ; Cato quia
multarum rerum usum habebat, et multa eius et in
10 Senatu et in foro vel provisa prudenter vel acta
constanter vel responsa acute ferebantur ; propterea
quasi cognomen iam habebat in senectute sapientis.
7. Te autem alio quodam modo, non solum natura
et moribus, verum etiam studio et doctrina esse
15 sapientem, nec sicut vulgus, sed ut eruditi solent
appellare sapientem, qualem in reliqua Graecia
neminem, —nam qui septem appellantur, eos qui ista
subtilius quaerunt in numero sapientium non habent
—Athenis unum accepimus et eum quidem etiam
20 Apollinis oraculo sapientissimum iudicatum ; hanc
esse in te sapientiam existimant ut omnia tua in te
posita esse ducas humanosque casus virtute inferiores putes.　Itaque ex me quaerunt, credo item
ex hoc Scaevola, quonam pacto mortem Africani
25 feras ; eoque magis quod his proximis Nonis, cum
in hortos D. Bruti auguris commentandi causa, ut
assolet, venissemus, tu non adfuisti qui diligentissime
semper illum diem et illud munus solitus esses obire.
　　8. SCAEVOLA.　Quaerunt quidem, C. Laeli,
30 multi, ut est a Fannio dictum ; sed ego id respondeo
quod animum adverti, te dolorem quem acceperis
cum summi viri tum amicissimi morte ferre moderate ; nec potuisse non commoveri, nec fuisse id
humanitatis tuae ; quod autem his Nonis in collegio

SOCRATES (*Bust in the Villa Albani*)
Note the prominent eyes, snub nose, and thick lips, which
were characteristic of him.

SILVER COIN OF CROTON (S. ITALY), 6TH
CENTURY B.C.

showing the tripod of Apollo from which
the oracles were delivered by the Pythian
priestess. It consisted of a three-legged
stand, supporting a cauldron. The legs
have lion's feet.

SILVER COIN OF ZACYNTHUS (WESTERN GREECE)
showing the head of Apollo with wreath, and the sacred
Apolline tripod.

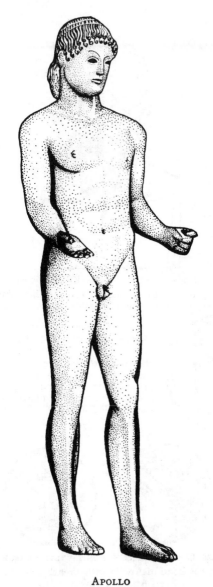

APOLLO

Bronze statuette, copied from a famous statue of Apollo at Branchidae near Miletus.

nostro non adfuisses valetudinem respondeo causam, 35 non maestitiam fuisse.

LAELIUS. Recte tu quidem, Scaevola, et vere. Nec enim ab isto officio quod semper usurpavi cum valerem abduci incommodo meo debui, nec ullo casu arbitror hoc constanti homini posse contingere 40 ut ulla intermissio fiat officii. 9. Tu autem, Fanni, quod mihi tantum tribui dicis, quantum ego nec agnosco nec postulo, facis amice; sed, ut mihi videris, non recte iudicas de Catone. Aut enim nemo, quod quidem magis credo, aut si quisquam, 45 ille sapiens fuit. Quomodo, ut alia omittam, mortem filii tulit! Memineram Paulum, videram Gallum; sed hi in pueris, Cato in perfecto et spectato viro. 10. Quam ob rem cave Catoni anteponas ne istum quidem ipsum quem Apollo, 50 ut ais, sapientissimum iudicavit. Huius enim facta, illius dicta laudantur. De me autem, ut iam cum utroque vestrum loquar, sic habetote.

CHAPTER III

I should lie if I denied feeling his loss; but I find consolation in the fact that no harm has happened to him and that he died after a most brilliant career when he had received every mark of honour from his grateful country.

Ego si Scipionis desiderio me moveri negem, quam id recte faciam viderint sapientes; sed certe mentiar. Moveor enim tali amico orbatus, qualis,

ut arbitror, nemo unquam erit, ut confirmare possum,
5 nemo certe fuit. Sed non egeo medicina ; me ipse
consolor et maxime illo solacio, quod eo errore careo
quo amicorum decessu plerique angi solent. Nihil
mali accidisse Scipioni puto ; mihi accidit si quid
accidit. Suis autem incommodis graviter angi non
10 amicum, sed se ipsum amantis est.

11. Cum illo vero quis neget actum esse praeclare? Nisi enim, quod ille minime putabat, im-
mortalitatem optare vellet, quid non est adeptus
quod homini fas esset optare? qui summam spem
15 civium, quam de eo iam puero habuerant, continuo
adulescens incredibili virtute superavit ; qui con-
sulatum petivit nunquam, factus est consul bis ;
primum ante tempus, iterum sibi suo tempore, rei
publicae paene sero ; qui duabus urbibus eversis
20 inimicissimis huic imperio non modo praesentia,
verum etiam futura bella delevit. Quid dicam de
moribus facillimis, de pietate in matrem, liberalitate
in sorores, bonitate in suos, iustitia in omnes?
Nota sunt vobis. Quam autem civitati carus
25 fuerit, maerore funeris indicatum est. Quid igitur
hunc paucorum annorum accessio iuvare potuisset?
Senectus enim quamvis non sit gravis, ut memini
Catonem anno ante quam mortuus est, mecum et
cum Scipione disserere, tamen aufert eam viriditatem
30 in qua etiamnunc erat Scipio.

12. Quam ob rem vita quidem talis fuit vel
fortuna vel gloria ut nihil posset accedere : moriendi
autem sensum celeritas abstulit. Quo de genere
mortis difficile dictu est ; quid homines suspicentur
videtis. Hoc vere tamen licet dicere, P. Scipioni 35
ex multis diebus quos in vita celeberrimos laetis-
simosque viderit, illum diem clarissimum fuisse,
cum Senatu dimisso domum reductus ad vesperum
est a patribus conscriptis, populo Romano, sociis
et Latinis, pridie quam excessit e vita, ut ex tam 40
alto dignitatis gradu ad superos videatur deos potius
quam ad inferos pervenisse.

CHAPTER IV

I believe with many others that the soul is immortal and that
Scipio has journeyed to the gods. Furthermore, the
recollection of our friendship and the hope that it will
become famous, are a great consolation to me.
FANNIUS : *Please give us, then, a talk on friendship.*

13. Neque enim assentior eis qui haec nuper
disserere coeperunt, cum corporibus simul animos
interire atque omnia morte deleri. Plus apud
me antiquorum auctoritas valet, vel nostrorum
maiorum qui mortuis tam religiosa iura tribuerunt, 5
quod non fecissent profecto, si nihil ad eos pertinere
arbitrarentur, vel eorum qui in hac terra fuerunt
magnamque Graeciam, quae nunc quidem deleta

est, tunc florebat, institutis et praeceptis suis
10 erudierunt; vel eius qui Apollinis oraculo sapi-
entissimus est iudicatus, qui non tur hoc, tum
illud, ut in plerisque, sed idem semр̤ur, animos
hominum esse divinos, eisque cum ex corpore
excessissent, reditum in caelum patere optimoque
15 et iustissimo cuique expeditissimum.

14. Quod idem Scipioni videbatur qui quidem,
quasi praesagiret, perpaucis ante mortem diebus,
cum et Philus et Manilius adesset et alii plures,
tuque etiam, Scaevola, mecum venisses, triduum
20 disseruit de re publica; cuius disputationis fuit
extremum fere de immortalitate animorum, quae
se in quiete per visum ex Africano audisse dicebat.
Id si ita est ut optimi cuiusque animus in morte
facillime evolet tamquam e custodia vinculisque
25 corporis, cui censemus cursum ad deos faciliorem
fuisse quam Scipioni? Quocirca maerere hoc eius
eventu vereor ne invidi magis quam amici sit. Sin
autem illa veriora ut idem interitus sit animorum
et corporum nec ullus sensus maneat, ut nihil boni
30 est in morte, sic certe nihil mali. Sensu enim
amisso, fit idem quasi natus non esset omnino;
quem tamen esse natum et nos gaudemus et haec
civitas dum erit laetabitur.

15. Quam ob rem cum illo quidem, ut supra
35 dixi, actum optime est, mecum incommodius, quem

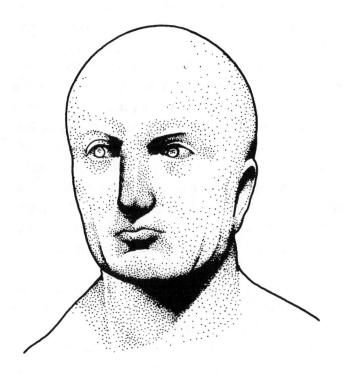

SCIPIO AFRICANUS MAJOR
*Bust in the Capitoline Museum generally identified
with Scipio.*

fuerat aequius, ut prius introieram, sic prius exire
de vita. Sed tamen recordatione nostrae amicitiae
sic fruor ut beate vixisse videar, quia cum Scipione
vixerim ; quocum mihi coniuncta cura de re
40 publica et de privata fuit, quocum et domus fuit
et militia communis, et id in quo est omnis vis
amicitiae, voluntatum, studiorum, sententiarum
summa consensio. Itaque non tam ista me sapientiae quam modo Fannius commemoravit fama
45 delectat, falsa praesertim, quam quod amicitiae
nostrae memoriam spero sempiternam fore. Idque
mihi eo magis est cordi quod ex omnibus saeculis
vix tria aut quattuor nominantur paria amicorum,
quo in genere sperare videor Scipionis et Laeli
50 amicitiam notam posteritati fore.

16. FANN. Istuc quidem, Laeli, ita necesse est.
Sed quoniam amicitiae mentionem fecisti et sumus
otiosi, pergratum mihi feceris, spero item Scaevolae,
si quem ad modum soles de ceteris rebus cum ex te
55 quaeruntur, sic de amicitia disputaris quid sentias,
qualem existimes, quae praecepta des.

SCAEV. Mihi vero erit gratum ; atque id ipsum
cum tecum agere conarer, Fannius antevertit. Quam
ob rem utrique nostrum gratum admodum feceris.

CHAPTER V

Laelius first emphasises his incapacity for the task, then begins:
Friendship can exist only between the good. The latter
are not confined to that imaginary class of super-beings,
the ' wise-men ' of the Stoics, but includes all those who
are commonly acknowledged to possess good and noble
qualities. Friendship is the strongest of the ties which
exist among mankind.

17. LAEL. Ego vero non gravarer, si mihi ipse
confiderem ; nam et praeclara res est, et sumus, ut
dixit Fannius, otiosi. Sed quis ego sum aut quae
est in me facultas? Doctorum est ista consuetudo
eaque Graecorum, ut eis ponatur de quo disputent 5
quamvis subito. Magnum opus est egetque exer-
citatione non parva. Quam ob rem quae disputari
de amicitia possunt, ab eis censeo petatis qui ista
profitentur. Ego vos hortari tantum possum ut
amicitiam omnibus rebus humanis anteponatis ; 10
nihil est enim tam naturae aptum, tam conveniens
ad res vel secundas vel adversas.

18. Sed hoc primum sentio nisi in bonis
amicitiam esse non posse ; neque id ad vivum
reseco, ut illi qui haec subtilius disserunt, fortasse 15
vere, sed ad communem utilitatem parum ; negant
enim quemquam virum bonum esse nisi sapientem.
Sit ita sane ; sed eam sapientiam interpretantur
quam adhuc mortalis nemo est consecutus. Nos

20 autem ea quae sunt in usu vitaque communi, non
ea quae finguntur aut optantur, spectare debemus.
Nunquam ego dicam C. Fabricium, M'. Curium,
Ti. Coruncanium, quos sapientes nostri maiores
iudicabant, ad istorum normam fuisse sapientes.
25 Qua re sibi habeant sapientiae nomen et invidiosum
et obscurum ; concedant ut hi boni viri fuerint.
Ne id quidem facient ; negabunt id nisi sapienti
posse concedi. 19. Agamus igitur pingui Minerva,
ut aiunt. Qui ita se gerunt, ita vivunt, ut eorum
30 probetur fides, integritas, aequitas, liberalitas, nec
sit in eis ulla cupiditas, libido, audacia, sintque
magna constantia, ut ei fuerunt modo quos nomi-
navi, hos viros bonos, ut habiti sunt, sic etiam
appellandos putemus, quia sequantur quantum
35 homines possunt naturam optimam bene vivendi
ducem.

Sic enim mihi perspicere videor, ita natos esse
nos ut inter omnes esset societas quaedam, maior
autem, ut quisque proxime accederet. Itaque
40 cives potiores quam peregrini, propinqui quam
alieni : cum his enim amicitiam natura ipsa peperit,
sed ea non satis habet firmitatis. Namque hoc
praestat amicitia propinquitati quod ex propinquitate benevolentia tolli potest, ex amicitia non
45 potest : sublata enim benevolentia amicitiae nomen
tollitur, propinquitatis manet. 20. Quanta autem

vis amicitiae sit ex hoc intellegi maxime potest,
quod ex infinita societate generis humani, quam
conciliavit ipsa natura, ita contracta res est et
adducta in angustum ut omnis caritas aut inter duos 50
aut inter paucos iungeretur.

CHAPTER VI

*Friendship is an accord in all things, human and divine,
allied with goodwill and affection : it is heaven's greatest
gift to man. It brings with it many advantages both in
prosperity and in adversity.*

Est autem amicitia nihil aliud nisi omnium
divinarum humanarumque rerum cum benevolentia
et caritate consensio ; qua quidem haud scio an
excepta sapientia nil unquam melius homini sit a
dis immortalibus datum. Divitias alii praeponunt, 5
bonam alii valetudinem, alii potentiam, alii honores,
multi etiam voluptates. Beluarum hoc quidem
extremum ; illa autem superiora caduca et incerta,
posita non tam in consiliis nostris quam in fortunae
temeritate. Qui autem in virtute summum bonum 10
ponunt, praeclare illi quidem, sed haec ipsa virtus
amicitiam et gignit et continet, nec sine virtute
amicitia esse ullo pacto potest. 21. Iam virtutem
ex consuetudine vitae sermonisque nostri interpretemur, nec eam, ut quidam docti, verborum 15
magnificentia metiamur, virosque bonos eos qui

habentur numeremus, Paulos, Catones, Gallos,
Scipiones, Philos : his communis vita contenta est :
eos autem omittamus qui omnino nusquam reperi-
20 untur. Tales igitur inter viros amicitia tantas
opportunitates habet quantas vix queo dicere.

22. Principio, qui potest esse vita vitalis, ut
ait Ennius, quae non in amici mutua benevolentia
conquiescat? Quid dulcius quam habere quicum
25 omnia audeas sic loqui ut tecum? Qui esset tantus
fructus in prosperis rebus, nisi haberes qui illis
aeque ac tu ipse gauderet? Adversas vero ferre
difficile esset sine eo qui illas gravius etiam quam
tu ferret. Denique ceterae res quae expetuntur
30 opportunae sunt singulae rebus fere singulis ;
divitiae ut utare ; opes ut colare ; honores ut
laudere ; voluptates ut gaudeas ; valetudo ut
dolore careas et muneribus fungare corporis :
amicitia res plurimas continet. Quoquo te verteris
35 praesto est : nullo loco excluditur : nunquam
intempestiva, nunquam molesta est. Itaque non
aqua, non igni, ut aiunt, locis pluribus utimur quam
amicitia. Neque ego nunc de vulgari aut de medio-
cri, quae tamen ipsa et delectat et prodest, sed de
40 vera et perfecta loquor, qualis eorum qui pauci
nominantur fuit. Nam et secundas res splendidiores
facit amicitia, et adversas partiens communicansque
leviores.

CHAPTER VII

Friendship stimulates men's hopes and maintains their spirits; without it no country, no city could exist. Empedocles taught that friendship unites the universe.

23. Cumque plurimas et maximas commoditates amicitia contineat, tum illa nimirum praestat omnibus, quod bonam spem praelucet in posterum nec debilitari animos aut cadere patitur. Verum enim amicum qui intuetur, tamquam exemplar 5 aliquod intuetur sui. Quocirca et absentes adsunt et egentes abundant et imbecilli valent, et, quod difficilius dictu est, mortui vivunt ; tantus eos honos, memoria, desiderium prosequitur amicorum, ex quo illorum beata mors videtur, horum vita 10 laudabilis. Quod si exemeris ex rerum natura benevolentiae coniunctionem, nec domus ulla nec urbs stare poterit ; ne agri quidem cultus permanebit. Id si minus intellegitur, quanta vis amicitiae concordiaeque sit ex dissensionibus atque 15 discordiis percipi potest. Quae enim domus tam stabilis, quae tam firma civitas est, quae non odiis atque discidiis funditus possit everti? ex quo quantum boni sit in amicitia iudicari potest.

24. Agrigentinum quidem doctum quendam 20 virum carminibus Graecis vaticinatum ferunt, quae in rerum natura totoque mundo constarent quaeque

moverentur, ea contrahere amicitiam, dissipare
discordiam. Atque hoc quidem omnes mortales
25 et intellegunt et re probant. Itaque si quando
aliquod officium exstitit amici in periculis aut
adeundis aut communicandis, quis est qui id non
maximis efferat laudibus? Qui clamores tota cavea
nuper in hospitis et amici mei M. Pacuvii nova
30 fabula ; cum ignorante rege uter esset Orestes,
Pylades Orestem se esse diceret, ut pro illo necare-
tur ; Orestes autem, ita ut erat, Orestem se esse
perseveraret. Stantes plaudebant in re ficta : quid
arbitramur in vera facturos fuisse? Facile indicabat
35 ipsa natura vim suam, cum homines quod facere
ipsi non possent id recte fieri in altero iudicarent.
Hactenus mihi videor de amicitia quid sentirem
potuisse dicere. Si quae praeterea sunt, credo
autem esse multa, ab eis, si videbitur, qui ista
40 disputant quaeritote.

FANNIUS : ' *Pray continue your dissertation, Laelius. No
one can do it better.'*

25. FANN. Nos autem a te potius : quamquam
etiam ab istis saepe quaesivi et audivi non invitus
equidem, sed aliud quoddam filum orationis tuae.

SCAEV. Tum magis id diceres, Fanni, si nuper
45 in hortis Scipionis, cum est de re publica disputatum, adfuisses. Qualis tum patronus iustitiae
fuit contra accuratam orationem Phili!

A Silver Coin of Agrigentum, end of 5th Century B.C.
The Charioteer is the chief type of Sicilian coins.

Attic Vase Painting, early 5th Century B.C.
representing the murder of Aegisthus by Orestes in revenge for his
father's murder.

FANN. Facile id quidem fuit iustitiam iustissimo viro defendere. SCAEV. Quid amicitiam? 50 Nonne facile ei, qui ob eam summa fide constantia iustitiaque servatam maximam gloriam ceperit?

CHAPTER VIII

LAELIUS: *I have often wondered whether it is the feeling of weakness or the need of help that makes men long for friendship, or whether there is a deeper and more beautiful reason—natural inclination. I incline to the latter rather than to that view which thinks of friendship in terms of profit and advantage.*

Two facts support this : (i) the feelings of love among animals and more so amongst men. (ii) the loveableness of virtue which wins our affection even in the case of men whom we have never seen.

26. LAEL. Vim hoc quidem est adferre. Quid enim refert qua me ratione cogatis? Cogitis certe : studiis enim generorum, praesertim in re bona, cum difficile est tum ne aequum quidem obsistere.

5 Saepissime igitur mihi de amicitia cogitanti maxime illud considerandum videri solet, utrum propter imbecillitatem atque inopiam desiderata sit amicitia, ut dandis recipiendisque meritis, quod quisque minus per se ipse posset, id acciperet ab 10 alio vicissimque redderet, an esset hoc quidem proprium amicitiae, sed antiquior et pulchrior et

magis a natura ipsa profecta alia causa. Amor
enim, ex quo amicitia nominata est, princeps
est ad benevolentiam coniungendam. Nam utilitates quidem etiam ab eis percipiuntur saepe 15
qui simulatione amicitiae coluntur et observantur
temporis causa : in amicitia autem nihil fictum
est, nihil simulatum ; et quidquid est, id et verum
est et voluntarium. 27. Quapropter a natura
mihi videtur potius quam ab indigentia orta ami- 20
citia, applicatione magis animi cum quodam sensu
amandi quam cogitatione quantum illa res utilitatis
esset habitura. Quod quidem quale sit etiam in
bestiis quibusdam animadverti potest, quae ex
se natos ita amant ad quoddam tempus et ab 25
eis ita amantur ut facile earum sensus appareat.
Quod in homine multo est evidentius : primum ex
ea caritate quae est inter natos et parentes, quae
dirimi nisi detestabili scelere non potest : deinde,
cum similis sensus exstitit amoris, si aliquem nacti 30
sumus cuius cum moribus et natura congruamus,
quod in eo quasi lumen aliquod probitatis et virtutis
perspicere videamur. 28. Nihil est enim amabilius
virtute, nihil quod magis adliciat ad diligendum,
quippe cum propter virtutem et probitatem etiam 35
eos quos nunquam vidimus quodam modo diligamus.
Quis est qui C. Fabrici, M'. Curi non cum caritate
aliqua et benevolentia memoriam usurpet, quos

nunquam viderit? Quis autem est qui Tarquinium
Superbum, qui Sp. Cassium, Sp. Maelium non 40
oderit? Cum duobus ducibus de imperio in Italia
decertatum est, Pyrrho et Hannibale. Ab altero
propter probitatem eius non nimis alienos animos
habemus; alterum propter crudelitatem semper
haec civitas oderit. 45

CHAPTER IX

*Friendship, then, arises from a natural inclination, stimulated
by our admiration for a friend's virtues, and by his service
and care on our behalf.*

*Thus, the desire of advantage is not the source of friend-
ship—witness the friendship between Scipio and myself.*

*We ignore the objections of those who judge everything
by the standard of pleasure.*

29. Quod si tanta vis probitatis est ut eam vel
in eis quos nunquam vidimus, vel, quod maius est,
in hoste etiam diligamus, quid mirum est si animi
hominum moveantur, cum eorum quibuscum usu
coniuncti esse possunt virtutem et bonitatem 5
perspicere videantur? Quamquam confirmatur amor
et beneficio accepto et studio perspecto et consuetudine adiuncta; quibus rebus ad illum primum
motum animi et amoris adhibitis admirabilis
quaedam exardescit benevolentiae magnitudo. 10
Quam si qui putant ab imbecillitate proficisci,

ut sit per quem adsequatur quod quisque desideret,
humilem sane relinquunt et minime generosum,
ut ita dicam, ortum amicitiae quam ex inopia
15 atque indigentia natam volunt. Quod si ita esset,
ut quisque minimum in se esse arbitraretur, ita
ad amicitiam esset aptissimus : quod longe secus
est. 30. Ut enim quisque sibi plurimum confidit
et ut quisque maxime virtute et sapientia sic
20 munitus est ut nullo egeat suaque omnia in se
ipso posita iudicet, ita in amicitiis expetendis
colendisque maxime excellit. Quid enim? Africanus indigens mei? Minime hercle : ac ne ego
quidem illius ; sed ego admiratione quadam virtutis
25 eius, ille vicissim opinione fortasse non nulla quam
de meis moribus habebat me dilexit ; auxit benevolentiam consuetudo. Sed quamquam utilitates
multae et magnae consecutae sunt, non sunt tamen
ab earum spe causae diligendi profectae. 31. Ut
30 enim benefici liberalesque sumus, non ut exigamus
gratiam, neque enim beneficium faeneramur, sed
natura propensi ad liberalitatem sumus ; sic amicitiam non spe mercedis adducti, sed quod omnis
eius fructus in ipso amore inest, expetendam
35 putamus.

  32. Ab his qui pecudum ritu ad voluptatem
omnia referunt longe dissentiunt : nec mirum.
Nihil enim altum, nihil magnificum ac divinum

suspicere possunt, qui suas omnes cogitationes ab-
iecerunt in rem tam humilem tamque contemptam. 40
Quam ob rem hos quidem ab hoc sermone removeamus, ipsi autem intellegamus natura gigni
sensum diligendi et benevolentiae caritatem facta
significatione probitatis ; quam qui appetiverunt
applicant se et propius admovent, ut et usu eius 45
quem diligere coeperunt fruantur et moribus,
sintque pares in amore et aequales, propensioresque
ad bene merendum quam ad reposcendum, atque
haec inter eos sit honesta certatio. Sic et utilitates
ex amicitia maximae capientur, et erit eius ortus 50
a natura quam ab imbecillitate et gravior et verior.
Nam si utilitas amicitias conglutinaret, eadem
commutata dissolveret. Sed quia natura mutari
non potest, idcirco verae amicitiae sempiternae
sunt. Ortum quidem amicitiae videtis, nisi quid 55
ad haec forte vultis.

FANN. Tu vero perge, Laeli. Pro hoc enim
qui minor est natu meo iure respondeo.

33. SCAEV. Recte tu quidem. Quam ob rem
audiamus. 60

BRONZE ETRUSCAN COIN OF THE END OF THE 3RD CENTURY B.C.
The head of the negro and the African elephant, no doubt,
refer to Hannibal's presence in Italy.

CHAPTER X

*The reasons which, according to Scipio, destroy friendship :
(i) a change of tastes, due to the passing of time ; (ii)
rivalry in love, money or political office ; (iii) the demanding of favours from friends contrary to morality.*

LAEL. Audite ergo, optimi viri, ea quae
saepissime inter me et Scipionem de amicitia
disserebantur. Quamquam ille quidem nihil difficilius esse dicebat quam amicitiam usque ad extre-
5 mum vitae diem permanere. Nam vel ut non
idem expediret incidere saepe, vel ut de re publica
non idem sentiretur : mutari etiam mores hominum
saepe dicebat, alias adversis rebus, alias aetate
ingravescente. Atque earum rerum exemplum ex
10 similitudine capiebat ineuntis aetatis, quod summi
puerorum amores saepe una cum praetexta toga
ponerentur : 34. sin autem ad adulescentiam perducti essent, dirimi tamen interdum contentione
vel uxoriae condicionis, vel commodi alicuius quod
15 idem adipisci uterque non posset. Quod si qui
longius in amicitia provecti essent, tamen saepe
labefactari, si in honoris contentionem incidissent :
pestem enim nullam maiorem esse in amicitiis
quam in plerisque pecuniae cupiditatem, in optimis
20 quibusque honoris certamen et gloriae ; ex quo inimicitias maximas saepe inter amicissimos exstitisse.

35. Magna etiam discidia et plerumque iusta
nasci, cum aliquid ab amicis quod rectum non
esset postularetur, ut aut libidinis ministri aut
adiutores essent ad iniuriam, quod qui recusarent, 25
quamvis honeste id facerent, ius tamen amicitiae
deserere arguerentur ab eis quibus obsequi nollent ;
illos autem, qui quidvis ab amico auderent postulare,
postulatione ipsa profiteri omnia se amici causa
esse facturos : eorum querella inveteratas non modo 30
familiaritates exstingui solere, sed etiam odia gigni
sempiterna. Haec ita multa quasi fata impendere
amicitiis ut omnia subterfugere non modo sapientiae,
sed etiam felicitatis diceret sibi videri.

CHAPTER XI

*How far affection should go in friendship. Examples from
history.*

36. Quam ob rem id primum videamus, si
placet, quatenus amor in amicitia progredi debeat.
Num, si Coriolanus habuit amicos, ferre contra
patriam arma illi cum Coriolano debuerunt? Num
Vecellinum amici regnum appetentem, num Maelium 5
debuerunt iuvare? 37. Ti. quidem Gracchum rem
publicam vexantem a Q. Tuberone aequalibusque
amicis derelictum videbamus. At C. Blossius Cumanus, hospes familiae vestrae, Scaevola, cum ad

10 me qui aderam Laenati et Rupilio consulibus in
consilio deprecatum venisset, hanc ut sibi ignoscerem
adferebat, quod tanti Ti. Gracchum fecisset ut
quidquid ille vellet sibi faciendum putaret. Tum
ego, 'Etiamne', inquam, 'si te in Capitolium
15 faces ferre vellet?' 'Nunquam voluisset id quidem.' 'Sed, si voluisset?' 'Paruissem.' Videtis
quam nefaria vox. Et hercle ita fecit, vel
plus etiam quam dixit; non enim paruit ille
Ti. Gracchi temeritati, sed praefuit, nec se comitem
20 illius furoris sed ducem praebuit. Itaque hac
amentia, quaestione nova perterritus, in Asiam
profugit, ad hostes se contulit, poenas rei publicae
graves iustasque persolvit.

Nulla est igitur excusatio peccati si amici
25 causa peccaveris; nam cum conciliatrix amicitiae
virtutis opinio fuerit, difficile est amicitiam manere
si a virtute defeceris. 38. Quod si rectum statuerimus vel concedere amicis quidquid velint vel
impetrare ab eis quidquid velimus, perfecta quidem
30 sapientia simus, si nihil habeat res viti : sed loquimur
de eis amicis qui ante oculos sunt, quos vidimus
aut de quibus memoriam accepimus, quos novit
vita communis. Ex hoc numero nobis exempla
sumenda sunt, et eorum quidem maxime qui ad
35 sapientiam proxime accedunt. 39. Videmus Papum
Aemilium C. Luscino familiarem fuisse; sic a

SILVER COIN OF PYRRHUS

Note the fine head of Zeus, who had a famous shrine in Epirus, and the inscription around the goddess Dione, ' of King Pyrrhus '.

ROMAN MEDALLION (END OF IST CENTURY A.D.)

Jupiter, holding his thunderbolt, stands between Minerva (on his right) and Juno. These three deities each had a division in the Capitoline temple.

ROMAN SILVER COIN ISSUED BY VOLTEIUS, ABOUT 78 B.C.

showing Jupiter Capitolinus on the obverse, and his temple on the Capitol on the reverse.

patribus accepimus, bis una consules, collegas in
censura : tum et cum eis et inter se coniunctissimos
fuisse M'. Curium et Ti. Coruncanium memoriae
40 proditum est. Igitur ne suspicari quidem possumus
quemquam horum ab amico quidpiam contendisse
quod contra fidem, contra ius iurandum, contra rem
publicam esset. Nam hoc quidem in talibus viris
quid attinet dicere, si contendisset impetraturum
45 non fuisse, cum illi sanctissimi viri fuerint, aeque
autem nefas sit tale aliquid et facere rogatum et
rogare? At vero Ti. Gracchum sequebantur C.
Carbo, C. Cato, et minime tunc quidem Gaius frater,
nunc idem acerrimus.

CHAPTER XII

First rule : neither make nor grant dishonourable requests.
More examples from politics and history.

40. Haec igitur lex in amicitia sanciatur ut
neque rogemus res turpes nec faciamus rogati.
Turpis enim excusatio est et minime accipienda
cum in ceteris peccatis, tum si quis contra rem
5 publicam se amici causa fecisse fateatur. Etenim
eo loco, Fanni et Scaevola, locati sumus ut nos
longe prospicere oporteat futuros casus rei publicae.
Deflexit iam aliquantulum de spatio curriculoque
consuetudo maiorum. Ti. Gracchus regnum occu-

pare conatus est, vel regnavit is quidem paucos 10
menses. 41. Num quid simile populus Romanus
audierat aut viderat? Hunc etiam post mortem
secuti amici et propinqui quid in P. Scipione
effecerint, sine lacrimis non queo dicere. Nam
Carbonem quoquo modo potuimus propter recentem 15
poenam Ti. Gracchi sustinuimus. De C. Gracchi
autem tribunatu quid exspectem non libet augurari.
Serpit enim in dies res, quae proclivis ad perniciem,
cum semel coepit labitur. Videtis in tabella iam
ante quanta facta sit labes, primo Gabinia lege, 20
biennio autem post Cassia. Videre iam videor
populum a senatu disiunctum, multitudinis arbitrio
res maximas agi. Plures enim discent quem ad
modum haec fiant, quam, quem ad modum his
resistatur. 42. Quorsum haec? Quia sine sociis 25
nemo quidquam tale conatur. Praecipiendum est
igitur bonis ut, si in eius modi amicitias ignari casu
aliquo inciderint, ne existiment ita se adligatos
ut ab amicis in magna aliqua re publica peccantibus
non discedant : improbis autem poena statuenda 30
est ; nec vero minor eis qui secuti erunt alterum,
quam eis qui ipsi fuerint impietatis duces. Quis
clarior in Graecia Themistocle? quis potentior?
qui cum imperator bello Persico servitute Graeciam
liberasset, propterque invidiam in exsilium expulsus 35
esset, ingratae patriae iniuriam non tulit quam

SILVER COIN

issued by Themistocles while in exile at Magnesia. On the obverse, inscribed ΘΕΜΙΣΤΟΚΛΕΟΣ is Apollo.

BRONZE COIN OF MAGNESIA (2ND CENTURY A.D.)

which probably represents the statue erected to Themistocles at Magnesia. Cf. the note on l. 39.

ferre debuit. Fecit idem quod xx annis ante apud
nos fecerat Coriolanus. His adiutor contra patriam
inventus est nemo : itaque mortem sibi uterque
conscivit. 43. Quare talis improborum consensio 40
non modo excusatione amicitiae tegenda non est,
sed potius supplicio omni vindicanda, ut ne quis
concessum putet amicum vel bellum patriae in-
ferentem sequi. Quod quidem, ut res coepit ire,
haud scio an aliquando futurum sit. Mihi autem 45
non minori curae est qualis res publica post mortem
meam futura sit, quam qualis hodie sit.

Chapter XIII

Let this law, then, be granted. A friend should be zealous,
frank, and outspoken. Here are examined and refuted
the opinions of certain Greek philosophers :

(i) close friendship should be shunned, to avoid worry
and anxiety : therefore hold loose to it and tighten or
slacken its ties at will.

(ii) we should seek friendship merely for advantage.

44. Haec igitur prima lex amicitiae sanciatur
ut ab amicis honesta petamus, amicorum causa
honesta faciamus ; ne exspectemus quidem dum
rogemur ; studium semper adsit, cunctatio absit :
consilium vero dare audeamus libere ; plurimum 5
in amicitia amicorum bene suadentium valeat
auctoritas, eaque et adhibeatur ad monendum

non modo aperte sed etiam acriter, si res postulabit,
et adhibitae pareatur. 45. Nam quibusdam, quos
10 audio sapientes habitos in Graecia, placuisse opinor
mirabilia quaedam (sed nihil est quod illi non
persequantur suis argutiis), partim fugiendas esse
nimias amicitias ne necesse sit unum sollicitum
esse pro pluribus ; satis superque esse suarum
15 cuique rerum, alienis nimis implicari molestum
esse : commodissimum esse quam laxissimas habenas
habere amicitiae, quas vel adducas cum velis vel
remittas ; caput enim esse ad beate vivendum
securitatem qua frui non possit animus, si tamquam
20 parturiat unus pro pluribus.
46. Alios autem dicere aiunt multo etiam
inhumanius, quem locum breviter paulo ante
perstrinxi, praesidii adiumentique causa, non benevolentiae neque caritatis, amicitias esse expetendas ;
25 itaque ut quisque minimum firmitatis habeat
minimumque virium, ita amicitias appetere maxime ;
ex eo fieri ut mulierculae magis amicitiarum prae-
sidia quaerant quam viri, et inopes quam opulenti,
et calamitosi quam ei qui putentur beati. 47. O
30 praeclaram sapientiam! Solem enim e mundo
tollere videntur qui amicitiam e vita tollunt, qua
nihil a dis immortalibus melius habemus, nihil
iucundius. Quae est enim ista securitas? · Specie
quidem blanda, sed reapse multis locis repudianda.

Neque enim est consentaneum ullam honestam 35
rem actionemve, ne sollicitus sis, aut non suscipere
aut susceptam deponere. Quod si curam fugimus,
virtus fugienda est, quae necesse est cum aliqua
cura res sibi contrarias aspernetur atque oderit,
ut bonitas malitiam, temperantia libidinem, igna- 40
viam fortitudo. Itaque videas rebus iniustis iustos
maxime dolere, imbellibus fortes, flagitiosis modes-
tos. Ergo hoc proprium est animi bene constituti
et laetari bonis rebus et dolere contrariis.

48. Quam ob rem si cadit in sapientem animi 45
dolor, qui profecto cadit, nisi ex eius animo ex-
stirpatam humanitatem arbitramur, quae causa
est cur amicitiam funditus tollamus e vita, ne
aliquas propter eam suscipiamus molestias? Quid
enim interest motu animi sublato, non dico 50
inter hominem et pecudem, sed inter hominem et
saxum aut truncum aut quidvis generis eiusdem?
Neque enim sunt isti audiendi qui virtutem duram
et quasi ferream esse quandam volunt ; quae
quidem est cum multis in rebus tum in amicitia 55
tenera atque tractabilis, ut et bonis amici quasi
diffundatur et incommodis contrahatur. Quam ob
rem angor iste qui pro amico saepe capiendus est
non tantum valet ut tollat e vita amicitiam, non
plus quam ut virtutes, quia non nullas curas et 60
molestias adferunt, repudientur.

Chapter XIV

Now friendship arises when virtue attracts a virtuous soul,
for it is the attraction of good men for good men, of like
for like. Friendship does not attend on advantage, but
advantage on friendship.

Cum autem contrahat amicitiam, ut supra dixi,
si qua significatio virtutis eluceat ad quam se
similis animus applicet et adiungat, id cum contigit,
amor exoriatur necesse est. 49. Quid enim tam
5 absurdum quam delectari multis inanibus rebus,
ut honore, ut gloria, ut aedificio, ut vestitu cultuque
corporis, animante virtute praedito, eo qui vel
amare, vel, ut ita dicam, redamare possit, non
admodum delectari? Nihil est enim remuneratione
10 benevolentiae, nihil vicissitudine studiorum offi-
ciorumque iucundius. 50. Quod si illud etiam
addimus, quod recte addi potest, nihil esse quod
ad se rem ullam tam adliciat et tam trahat quam
ad amicitiam similitudo, concedetur profecto verum
15 esse ut bonos boni diligant adsciscantque sibi quasi
propinquitate coniunctos atque natura. Nihil est
enim appetentius similium sui, nihil rapacius, quam
natura. Quam ob rem hoc quidem, Fanni et
Scaevola, constat, ut opinor, bonis inter bonos
20 quasi necessariam benevolentiam, qui est amicitiae
fons a natura constitutus. Sed eadem bonitas

etiam ad multitudinem pertinet. Non est enim
inhumana virtus neque immunis neque superba,
quae etiam populos universos tueri eisque optime
consulere soleat ; quod non faceret profecto, si a 25
caritate vulgi abhorreret.

51. Atque etiam mihi quidem videntur, qui
utilitatis causa fingunt amicitias, amabilissimum
nodum amicitiae tollere. Non enim tam utilitas
parta per amicum quam amici amor ipse delectat ; 30
tumque illud fit, quod ab amico est profectum,
iucundum, si cum studio est profectum ; tantumque
abest ut amicitiae propter indigentiam colantur, ut
ei qui opibus et copiis maximeque virtute praediti,
in qua plurimum est praesidii, minime alterius 35
indigeant, liberalissimi sint et beneficentissimi.
Atque haud scio an ne opus sit quidem nihil unquam
omnino deesse amicis. Ubi enim studia nostra
viguissent, si nunquam consilio, nunquam opera
nostra nec domi nec militiae Scipio eguisset? Non 40
igitur utilitatem amicitia, sed utilitas amicitiam
secuta est.

CHAPTER XV

*Who would prefer wealth and power, on condition that he
neither love nor be loved? Such is the life of tyrants, the
powerful and the rich who have no true or loyal friends.*

52. Non ergo erunt homines deliciis diffluentes
audiendi, si quando de amicitia quam nec usu nec

ratione habent cognitam disputabunt. Nam quis
est, pro deorum fidem atque hominum, qui velit,
5 ut neque diligat quemquam nec ipse ab ullo
diligatur, circumfluere omnibus copiis atque in
omnium rerum abundantia vivere? Haec enim
est tyrannorum vita, nimirum in qua nulla fides,
nulla caritas, nulla stabilis benevolentiae potest
10 esse fiducia ; omnia semper suspecta atque sollicita,
nullus locus amicitiae. 53. Quis enim aut eum
diligat quem metuat, aut eum a quo se metui putet?
Coluntur tamen simulatione dumtaxat ad tempus.
Quod si forte, ut fit plerumque, ceciderint, tum
15 intellegitur quam fuerint inopes amicorum. Quod
Tarquinium dixisse ferunt exsulantem tum se intellexisse quos fidos amicos habuisset, quos in-
fidos, cum iam neutris gratiam referre posset.

54. Quamquam miror, illa superbia et importu-
20 nitate, si quemquam habere potuit. Atque ut
huius, quem dixi, mores veros amicos parare non
potuerunt, sic multorum opes praepotentium ex-
cludunt amicitias fideles. Non enim solum ipsa
fortuna caeca est, sed eos etiam plerumque efficit
25 caecos quos complexa est. Itaque efferuntur fere
fastidio et contumacia, nec quicquam insipiente
fortunato intolerabilius fieri potest. Atque hoc
quidem videre licet, eos qui antea commodis fuerunt
moribus, imperio, potestate, prosperis rebus im-

mutari, sperni ab eis veteres amicitias, indulgeri 30
novis. 55. Quid autem stultius quam, cum plurimum copiis, facultatibus, opibus possint, cetera
parare quae parantur pecunia, equos, famulos,
vestem egregiam, vasa pretiosa ; amicos non parare,
optimam et pulcherrimam vitae, ut ita dicam, 35
supellectilem? Etenim cetera cum parant, cui
parent nesciunt, nec cuius causa laborent ; eius enim
est istorum quidque qui vicit viribus : amicitiarum
sua cuique permanet stabilis et certa possessio, ut
etiam si illa maneant, quae sunt quasi dona fortunae, 40
tamen vita inculta et deserta ab amicis non possit
esse iucunda. Sed haec hactenus.

Chapter XVI

What are the limits to be set to friendship? Three opinions
are stated, (i) to have the same feelings for our friends as
we have for ourselves ; (ii) to love them just as much as
they love us ; (iii) to be valued by our friends as we value
ourselves.

The first ignores the fact that we do for our friend what
we would not do for ourselves. The second is too cold and
calculating. The third ignores the duty of a friend to
cheer and inspire.

56. Constituendi autem sunt qui sint in amicitia
fines et quasi termini diligendi ; de quibus tres
video sententias ferri quarum nullam probo : unam,

ut eodem modo erga amicos adfecti simus quo erga
5 nosmet ipsos ; alteram, ut nostra in amicos benevolentia illorum erga nos benevolentiae pariter
aequaliterque respondeat ; tertiam, ut quanti quisque se ipse facit, tanti fiat ab amicis.   Harum trium
sententiarum nulli prorsus adsentior.   Nec enim
10 illa prima vera est ut quem ad modum in se quisque,
sic in amicum sit animatus. 57. Quam multa
enim   quae   nostra   causa   nunquam   faceremus,
facimus causa amicorum ;   precari ab indigno,
supplicare ; tum acerbius in aliquem invehi insec-
15 tarique vehementius ; quae in nostris rebus non
satis   honeste,   in   amicorum   fiunt   honestissime ;
multaeque res sunt in quibus de suis commodis
viri boni multa detrahunt detrahique patiuntur,
ut eis amici potius quam ipsi fruantur.   58. Altera
20 sententia est quae definit amicitiam paribus officiis
ac voluntatibus.   Hoc quidem est nimis exigue
et exiliter ad calculos vocare amicitiam, ut par sit
ratio acceptorum et datorum.   Divitior mihi et
adfluentior videtur esse vera amicitia, nec observare
25 restricte ne plus reddat quam acceperit.   Neque
enim verendum est ne quid excidat, aut ne quid
in terram defluat, aut ne plus aequo in amicitiam
congeratur.

59. Tertius vero ille finis deterrimus, ut quanti
30 quisque se ipse faciat, tanti fiat ab amicis.   Saepe

enim in quibusdam aut animus abiectior est aut
spes amplificandae fortunae fractior. Non est
igitur amici talem esse in eum qualis ille in se est,
sed potius eniti et efficere ut amici iacentem animum
excitet inducatque spem cogitationemque meliorem. 35
Alius igitur finis verae amicitiae constituendus est,
si prius, quid maxime reprehendere Scipio solitus
sit, dixero. Negabat ullam vocem inimiciorem
amicitiae potuisse reperiri quam eius qui dixisset
ita amare oportere ut si aliquando esset osurus ; 40
nec vero se adduci posse ut hoc, quem ad modum
putaretur, a Biante esse dictum crederet, qui
sapiens habitus esset unus e septem ; impuri cuius-
dam aut ambitiosi aut omnia ad suam potentiam
revocantis esse sententiam. Quonam enim modo 45
quisquam amicus esse poterit ei cui se putabit in-
imicum esse posse? Quin etiam necesse erit cupere
et optare ut quam saepissime peccet amicus, quo
plures det sibi tamquam ansas ad reprehendendum ;
rursum autem recte factis commodisque amicorum 50
necesse erit angi, dolere, invidere. 60. Qua re hoc
quidem praeceptum cuiuscunque est ad tollendam
amicitiam valet. Illud potius praecipiendum fuit,
ut eam diligentiam adhiberemus in amicitiis com-
parandis ut ne quando amare inciperemus eum quem 55
aliquando odisse possemus. Quin etiam si minus
felices in deligendo fuissemus, ferendum id Scipio

potius quam inimicitiarum tempus cogitandum
putabat.

CHAPTER XVII

What are the limits then?

(i) *We may support a friend, in extreme cases, even
though we deviate from the straight path, provided that
this does not involve us in disgrace.*

(ii) *Friends being the most important of possessions,
we should examine and test them more carefully than other
property, especially their behaviour in adversity.*

61. His igitur finibus utendum arbitror, ut
cum emendati mores amicorum sint, tum sit inter
eos omnium rerum, consiliorum, voluntatum sine
ulla exceptione communitas, ut etiam, si qua fortuna
5 acciderit ut minus iustae amicorum voluntates
adiuvandae sint in quibus eorum aut caput agatur
aut fama, declinandum sit de via, modo ne summa
turpitudo sequatur : est enim quatenus amicitiae
dari venia possit. Nec vero neglegenda est fama,
10 nec mediocre telum ad res gerendas existimare
oportet benevolentiam civium, quam blanditiis et
adsentando colligere turpe est ; virtus quam sequitur
caritas minime repudianda est.

62. Sed—saepe enim redeo ad Scipionem cuius
15 omnis sermo erat de amicitia,—querebatur quod
omnibus in rebus homines diligentiores essent ;

capras et oves quot quisque haberet dicere posse,
amicos quot haberet non posse dicere ; et in illis
quidem parandis adhibere curam, in amicis eligendis
neglegentes esse nec habere quasi signa quaedam 20
et notas quibus eos qui ad amicitiam essent idonei
iudicarent. Sunt igitur firmi et stabiles et con-
stantes eligendi, cuius generis est magna penuria,
et iudicare difficile est sane nisi expertum ; experien-
dum autem est in ipsa amicitia ; ita praecurrit 25
amicitia iudicium tollitque experiendi potestatem.
63. Est igitur prudentis sustinere ut cursum, sic
impetum benevolentiae, quo utamur, quasi equis
temptatis, sic amicitia ex aliqua parte periclitatis
moribus amicorum. Quidam saepe in parva pecunia 30
perspiciuntur quam sint leves : quidam, quos parva
movere non potuit, cognoscuntur in magna. Sin
erunt aliqui reperti qui pecuniam praeferre amicitiae
sordidum existiment, ubi eos inveniemus qui
honores, magistratus, imperia, potestates, opes ami- 35
citiae non anteponant, ut, cum ex altera parte
proposita haec sint, ex altera ius amicitiae, non
multo illa malint? Imbecilla enim natura est ad
contemnendam potentiam, quam etiam si neglecta
amicitia consecuti sunt, obscuratum iri arbitrantur, 40
quia non sine magna causa sit neglecta amicitia.
64. Itaque verae amicitiae difficillime reperiuntur
in eis qui in honoribus reque publica versantur.

Ubi enim istum invenias qui honorem amici ante-
45 ponat suo? Quid? haec ut omittam, quam graves,
quam difficiles plerisque videntur calamitatum
societates, ad quas non est facile inventu qui
descendant : quamquam Ennius recte :

Amicus certus in re incerta cernitur :

50 tamen haec duo levitatis et infirmitatis plerosque
convincunt, aut si in bonis rebus contemnunt, aut
in malis deserunt.

Qui igitur utraque in re gravem, constantem,
stabilem se in amicitia praestiterit, hunc ex maxime
55 raro hominum genere iudicare debemus et paene
divino.

Chapter XVIII

*As the most important quality in friendship is loyalty, we
should choose as friends, those who are frank, sociable,
sympathetic, and free from malice.*
    Two rules should be maintained :
    (i) *be free from hypocrisy ;*
    (ii) *avoid slander and suspicion.*

65. Firmamentum autem stabilitatis constantiaeque est eius quam in amicitia quaerimus fides.
Nihil enim stabile est quod infidum. Simplicem
praeterea et communem et consentientem qui rebus
5 isdem moveatur eligi par est ; quae omnia pertinent

ad fidelitatem. Neque enim fidum potest esse
multiplex ingenium et tortuosum ; neque vero, qui
non isdem rebus movetur naturaque consentit, aut
fidus aut stabilis potest esse. Addendum eodem
est ut ne criminibus aut inferendis delectetur aut 10
credat oblatis, quae pertinent omnia ad eam, quam
iamdudum tracto, constantiam. Ita fit verum illud,
quod initio dixi, amicitiam nisi inter bonos esse non
posse.

Est enim boni viri, quem eundem sapientem 15
licet dicere, haec duo tenere in amicitia ; primum,
ne quid fictum sit neve simulatum : aperte enim
vel odisse magis ingenui est quam fronte occultare
sententiam : deinde, non solum ab aliquo adlatas
criminationes repellere, sed ne ipsum quidem esse 20
suspiciosum, semper aliquid existimantem ab amico
esse violatum. 66. Accedat huc suavitas quaedam
oportet sermonum atque morum, haudquaquam
mediocre condimentum amicitiae. Tristitia autem
et in omni re severitas habet illa quidem gravitatem, 25
sed amicitia remissior esse debet et liberior et
dulcior et ad omnem comitatem facilitatemque
proclivior.

Chapter XIX

A difficult question : are new friends to be preferred to old
ones? No,—but new friends should not be rejected.
  Friends should all be on an equal footing : there should
be no superiors nor inferiors.

67. Existit autem hoc loco quaedam quaestio
subdifficilis : num quando amici novi, digni amicitia,
veteribus sint anteponendi, ut equis vetulis teneros
anteponere solemus. Indigna homine dubitatio.
5 Non enim amicitiarum debent esse, sicut aliarum
rerum, satietates. Veterrima quaeque, ut ea vina
quae vetustatem ferunt, esse debent suavissima :
verumque illud est quod dicitur, multos modios
salis simul edendos esse ut amicitiae munus expletum
10 sit. 68. Novitates autem si spem adferunt, ut
tamquam in herbis non fallacibus fructus appareat,
non sunt illae quidem repudiandae, vetustas tamen
suo loco conservanda : maxima est enim vis vetustatis et consuetudinis. Quin in ipso equo, cuius
15 modo mentionem feci, si nulla res impediat, nemo
est quin eo quo consuevit, libentius utatur quam
intractato et novo : nec vero in hoc quod est
animal, sed in eis etiam quae sunt inanima consuetudo valet, cum locis ipsis delectemur, montuosis
20 etiam et silvestribus, in quibus diutius commorati
sumus.

69. Sed maximum est in amicitia parem esse
inferiori ; saepe enim excellentiae quaedam sunt,
qualis erat Scipionis in nostro, ut ita dicam, grege.
Nunquam se ille Philo, nunquam Rupilio, nunquam 25
Mummio anteposuit, nunquam inferioris ordinis
amicis : Q. vero Maximum fratrem, egregium virum
omnino, sibi nequaquam parem, quod is anteibat
aetate, tamquam superiorem colebat, suosque omnes
per se posse esse ampliores volebat. 70. Quod 30
faciendum imitandumque est omnibus, ut, si quam
praestantiam virtutis, ingenii, fortunae consecuti
sint, impertiant ea suis communicentque cum
proximis ; ut, si parentibus nati sint humilibus,
si propinquos habeant imbecilliores vel animo vel 35
fortuna, eorum augeant opes eisque honori sint et
dignitati : ut in fabulis, qui aliquamdiu propter
ignorationem stirpis et generis in famulatu fuerint,
cum cogniti sunt et aut deorum aut regum filii
inventi, retinent tamen caritatem in pastores quod 40
patres multos annos esse duxerunt. Quod est multo
profecto magis in veris patribus certisque faciendum.
Fructus enim ingeni et virtutis omnisque praes-
tantiae tum maximus capitur, cum in proximum
quemque confertur. **45**

ROMANS PLAYING BALL

(*From a wall-painting*)

HUNTING SCENE

(*Roman Mosaic from Carthage*)

CHAPTER XX

Therefore, the superior must put themselves on an equality with their friends, while the inferior should not be indignant at any pre-eminence on the part of others.

Friends should be assisted as much as is possible and consistent with their position.

We should make friends in manhood, not early youth.

Finally, goodwill should not be so unrestrained as to injure a friend : therefore examine your own demands on others, and what they may demand of you.

71. Ut igitur ei qui sunt in amicitiae coniunctionisque necessitudine superiores, exaequare se cum inferioribus debent, sic inferiores non dolere se a suis aut ingenio aut fortuna aut dignitate
5 superari. Quorum plerique aut queruntur semper aliquid aut etiam exprobrant ; eoque magis, si habere se putant quod officiose et amice et cum labore aliquo suo factum queant dicere. Odiosum sane genus hominum officia exprobrantium, quae
10 meminisse debet is in quem collata sunt, non commemorare qui contulit. 72. Quam ob rem ut ei qui superiores sunt submittere se debent in amicitia, sic quodam modo inferiores extollere. Sunt enim quidam qui molestas amicitias faciunt, cum ipsi
15 se contemni putant ; quod non fere contingit nisi eis qui etiam contemnendos se arbitrantur, qui hac opinione non modo verbis sed etiam opere levandi

THE MURDER OF PRIAM, KING OF TROY, BY NEOPTOLEMUS
(Greek vase. About 480 B.C.)

sunt. 73. Tantum autem cuique tribuendum,
primum, quantum ipse efficere possis ; deinde etiam,
20 quantum ille quem diligas atque adiuves sustinere.
Non enim neque tu possis, quamvis excellas, omnes
tuos ad honores amplissimos perducere ; ut Scipio
P. Rupilium potuit consulem efficere, fratrem eius
Lucium non potuit. Quod si etiam possis quidvis
25 deferre ad alterum, videndum est tamen quid ille
possit sustinere.

74. Omnino amicitiae corroboratis iam con-
firmatisque et ingeniis et aetatibus iudicandae
sunt ; nec si qui ineunte aetate venandi aut pilae
30 studiosi fuerunt, eos habere necessarios quos tum
eodem studio praeditos dilexerunt ; isto enim
modo nutrices et paedagogi iure vetustatis plurimum
benevolentiae postulabunt. Qui neglegendi quidem
non sunt, sed alio quodam modo aestimandi : aliter
35 amicitiae stabiles permanere non possunt. Dis-
pares enim mores disparia studia sequuntur quorum
dissimilitudo dissociat amicitias ; nec ob aliam
causam ullam boni improbis, improbi bonis amici
esse non possunt, nisi quod tanta est inter eos,
40 quanta maxima potest esse, morum studiorumque
distantia.

75. Recte etiam praecipi potest in amicitiis ne
intemperata quaedam benevolentia, quod persaepe
fit, impediat magnas utilitates amicorum. Nec

45 enim, ut ad fabulas redeam, Troiam Neoptolemus
capere potuisset, si Lycomedem apud quem erat
educatus, multis cum lacrimis iter suum impedien-
tem, audire voluisset ; et saepe incidunt magnae
res ut discedendum sit ab amicis : quas qui im-
50 pedire vult, quod desiderium non facile ferat, is et
infirmus est mollisque natura et ob eam ipsam
causam in amicitia parum iustus. 76. Atque in
omni re considerandum est et quid postules ab
amico et quid patiare a te impetrari.

CHAPTER XXI

Friendships are broken : (i) *by faults on one side ;* (ii) *by*
change in tastes, due to the passing of time.

In the former case, they should be broken gradually, but
suddenly in bad cases. In the latter, estrangement
should not be allowed to develop into open enmity.

The best safeguard is care in the original choice.

Est etiam quasi quaedam calamitas in amicitiis
dimittendis non nunquam necessaria ; iam enim a
sapientium familiaritatibus ad vulgares amicitias
oratio nostra delabitur. Erumpunt saepe vitia
5 amicorum tum in ipsos amicos, tum in alienos,
quorum tamen ad amicos redundet infamia. Tales
igitur amicitiae sunt remissione usus eluendae et,
ut Catonem dicere audivi, dissuendae magis quam
discindendae ; nisi quaedam admodum intolerabilis

iniuria exarserit, ut neque rectum neque honestum 10
sit nec fieri possit ut non statim alienatio disiunctio-
que facienda sit.

77. Sin autem aut morum aut studiorum commutatio quaedam, ut fieri solet, facta erit, aut in
rei publicae partibus dissensio intercesserit, loquor 15
enim iam, ut paulo ante dixi, non de sapientium
sed de communibus amicitiis, cavendum erit ne
non solum amicitiae depositae sed etiam inimicitiae
susceptae videantur. Nihil enim turpius quam
cum eo bellum gerere quicum familiariter vixeris. 20
Ab amicitia Q. Pompei meo nomine se removerat,
ut scitis, Scipio ; propter dissensionem autem, quae
erat in re publica, alienatus est a collega nostro
Metello. Utrumque egit graviter ac moderate et
offensione animi non acerba. 78. Quam ob rem 25
primum danda opera est ne qua amicorum discidia
fiant ; sin tale aliquid evenerit, ut exstinctae
potius amicitiae quam oppressae esse videantur.
Cavendum vero ne etiam in graves inimicitias
convertant se amicitiae, ex quibus iurgia, maledicta, 30
contumeliae gignuntur. Quae tamen si tolerabiles
erunt, ferendae sunt, et hic honos veteri amicitiae
tribuendus, ut is in culpa sit qui faciat, non is qui
patiatur iniuriam.

Omnino omnium horum vitiorum atque in- 35
commodorum una cautio est atque una provisio,

ut ne nimis cito diligere incipiant neve non dignos.
79. Digni autem sunt amicitia quibus in ipsis inest
causa cur diligantur. Rarum genus, et quidem
40 omnia praeclara rara, nec quidquam difficilius quam
reperire quod sit omni ex parte in suo genere perfectum. Sed plerique neque in rebus humanis
quidquam bonum norunt nisi quod fructuosum sit,
et amicos tamquam pecudes eos potissimum diligunt
45 ex quibus sperant se maximum fructum esse
capturos. 80. Ita pulcherrima illa et maxime
naturali carent amicitia per se et propter se expetenda, nec ipsi sibi exemplo sunt, haec vis amicitiae
qualis et quanta sit. Ipse enim se quisque diligit,
50 non ut aliquam a se ipse mercedem exigat caritatis
suae, sed quod per se sibi quisque carus est. Quod
nisi idem in amicitiam transferetur, verus amicus nunquam reperietur; est enim is qui est tamquam alter
idem. 81. Quod si hoc apparet in bestiis, volucribus,
55 nantibus, agrestibus, cicuribus, feris, primum ut
se ipsae diligant, id enim pariter cum omni animante
nascitur, deinde ut requirant atque appetant ad
quas se applicent eiusdem generis animantes, idque
faciunt cum desiderio et cum quadam similitudine
60 amoris humani, quanto id magis in homine fit
natura, qui et se ipse diligit et alterum anquirit
cuius animum ita cum suo misceat ut efficiat paene
unum ex duobus?

Chapter XXII

We must not expect in friends virtues we do not possess ourselves.

Friendship is not to be regarded as an opportunity for passion or sin.

Affection should follow judgment, not vice versa.

82. Sed plerique perverse, ne dicam impudenter, habere talem amicum volunt quales ipsi esse non possunt ; quaeque ipsi non tribuunt amicis, haec ab eis desiderant. Par est autem primum ipsum esse virum bonum, tum alterum similem sui quaerere. 5 In talibus ea, quam iamdudum tractamus, stabilitas amicitiae confirmari potest, cum homines benevolentia coniuncti primum cupiditatibus eis quibus ceteri serviunt imperabunt ; deinde aequitate iustitiaque gaudebunt omniaque alter pro altero sus- 10 cipiet ; neque quicquam unquam nisi honestum et rectum alter ab altero postulabit, neque solum colent inter se ac diligent sed etiam verebuntur. Nam maximum ornamentum amicitiae tollit qui ex ea tollit verecundiam. 83. Itaque in eis pernici- 15 osus est error qui existimant libidinum peccatorumque omnium patere in amicitia licentiam. Virtutum amicitia adiutrix a natura data est, non vitiorum comes, ut, quoniam solitaria non posset virtus ad ea quae summa sunt pervenire, coniuncta et con- 20

sociata cum altera perveniret. Quae si quos inter
societas aut est aut fuit aut futura est, eorum est
habendus ad summum naturae bonum optimus
beatissimusque comitatus. 84. Haec est, inquam,
25 societas in qua omnia insunt quae putant homines
expetenda, honestas, gloria, tranquillitas animi
atque iucunditas, ut et, cum haec adsint, beata
vita sit, et sine his esse non possit.

Quod cum optimum maximumque sit, si id
30 volumus adipisci, virtuti opera danda est, sine qua
nec amicitiam neque ullam rem expetendam con-
sequi possumus : ea vero neglecta, qui se amicos
habere arbitrantur, tum se denique errasse sentiunt
cum eos gravis aliquis casus experiri cogit. 85.
35 Quocirca, dicendum est enim saepius, cum iudicaris, diligere oportet ; non, cum dilexeris, iudicare.
Sed cum multis in rebus neglegentia plectimur,
tum maxime in amicis et deligendis et colendis ;
praeposteris enim utimur consiliis et acta agimus,
40 quod vetamur vetere proverbio. Nam, implicati
ultro et citro vel usu diuturno vel etiam officiis,
repente in medio cursu amicitias exorta aliqua
offensione dirumpimus.

Chapter XXIII

*In nothing else is carelessness so blameworthy. For all men
agree on the value of friendship. Heaven itself would be
dull without a friend.*

86. Quo etiam magis vituperanda est rei
maxime necessariae tanta incuria. Una est enim
amicitia in rebus humanis de cuius utilitate omnes
uno ore consentiunt : quamquam a multis ipsa
virtus contemnitur et venditatio quaedam atque 5
ostentatio esse dicitur. Multi divitias despiciunt,
quos parvo contentos tenuis victus cultusque
delectat ; honores vero quorum cupiditate quidam
inflammantur, quam multi ita contemnunt ut
nihil inanius, nihil esse levius existiment. Itemque 10
cetera quae quibusdam admirabilia videntur, permulti sunt qui pro nihilo putent. De amicitia
omnes ad unum idem sentiunt, et ei qui ad rem
publicam se contulerunt, et ei qui rerum cognitione
doctrinaque delectantur, et ei qui suum negotium 15
gerunt otiosi, postremo ei qui se totos tradiderunt
voluptatibus, sine amicitia vitam esse nullam, si
modo velint aliqua ex parte liberaliter vivere.
87. Serpit enim nescio quomodo per omnium vitas
amicitia, nec ullam aetatis degendae rationem 20
patitur esse expertem sui.

Quin etiam si quis asperitate ea est et immani-

tate naturae, congressus ut hominum fugiat atque
oderit, qualem fuisse Athenis Timonem nescio
quem accepimus, tamen is pati non possit ut non 25
anquirat aliquem apud quem evomat virus acerbi-
tatis suae. Atque hoc maxime iudicaretur, si quid
tale posset contingere ut aliquis nos deus ex hac
hominum frequentia tolleret et in solitudine uspiam
collocaret atque ibi suppeditans omnium rerum 30
quas natura desiderat abundantiam et copiam,
hominis omnino adspiciendi potestatem eriperet.
Quis tam esset ferreus qui eam vitam ferre posset,
cuique non auferret fructum voluptatum omnium
solitudo? 88. Verum ergo illud est quod a Taren- 35
tino Archyta, ut opinor, dici solitum, nostros senes
commemorare audivi ab aliis senibus auditum :
si quis in caelum ascendisset naturamque mundi
et pulchritudinem siderum perspexisset, insuavem
illam admirationem ei fore, quae iucundissima 40
fuisset si aliquem cui narraret habuisset. Sic
natura solitarium nihil amat, semperque ad aliquod
tamquam adminiculum adnititur, quod in amicissimo quoque dulcissimum est.

Chapter XXIV

*To advise and rebuke, though often the cause of offence, are the
duty of friends ; but we must be careful to avoid harshness
or insult.*

*Flattery and complaisance ruin many, who cannot, or
will not hear the truth, but are vexed at correction and
admonition.*

Sed cum tot signis eadem natura declaret
quid velit, anquirat, desideret, obsurdescimus tamen
nescio quomodo, nec ea quae ab ea monemur
audimus. Est enim varius et multiplex usus
5 amicitiae multaeque causae suspicionum offensi-
onumque dantur, quas tum evitare, tum elevare,
tum ferre sapientis est. Una illa subeunda offensio
est ut et utilitas in amicitia et fides retineatur ;
nam et monendi amici saepe sunt et obiurgandi ;
10 et haec accipienda amice cum benevole fiunt.
89. Sed nescio quomodo verum est, quod in Andria
familiaris meus dicit :

Obsequium amicos, veritas odium parit.

Molesta veritas, si quidem ex ea nascitur odium,
15 quod est venenum amicitiae ; sed obsequium multo
molestius, quod peccatis indulgens praecipitem
amicum ferri sinit ; maxima autem culpa in eo
qui et veritatem aspernatur et in fraudem obsequio
impellitur.

20 Omni igitur hac in re habenda ratio et diligentia
est, primum, ut monitio acerbitate, deinde ut

obiurgatio contumelia careat. In obsequio autem, quoniam Terentiano verbo lubenter utimur, comitas adsit, assentatio vitiorum adiutrix procul amoveatur, quae non modo amico sed ne libero quidem 25 digna est : aliter enim cum tyranno, aliter cum amico vivitur. 90. Cuius autem aures veritati clausae sunt ut ab amico verum audire nequeat, huius salus desperanda est. Scitum est enim illud Catonis, ut multa : melius de quibusdam acerbos 30 inimicos mereri quam eos amicos qui dulces videantur ; illos verum saepe dicere, hos nunquam. Atque illud absurdum est, quod ei qui monentur eam molestiam quam debent capere non capiunt, eam capiunt qua debent vacare. Peccasse enim se non 35 anguntur ; obiurgari moleste ferunt ; quod contra oportebat delicto dolere, correctione gaudere.

CHAPTER XXV

The mischief of flattery, and its failures in action.

91. Ut igitur et monere et moneri proprium est verae amicitiae, et alterum libere facere, non aspere, alterum patienter accipere, non repugnanter, sic habendum est nullam in amicitiis pestem esse maiorem quam adulationem, blanditiam, assenta- 5 tionem : quamvis enim multis nominibus est hoc vitium notandum levium hominum atque fallacium, ad voluptatem loquentium omnia, nihil ad veritatem. 92. Cum autem omnium rerum simulatio

10 vitiosa est, tollit enim iudicium veri idque adulterat,
tum amicitiae repugnat maxime ; delet enim
veritatem sine qua nomen amicitiae valere non
potest. Nam cum amicitiae vis sit in eo ut unus
quasi animus fiat ex pluribus, qui id fieri poterit,
15 si ne in uno quidem quoque unus animus erit
idemque semper, sed varius, commutabilis, multiplex? 93. Quid enim potest esse tam flexibile,
tam devium, quam animus eius qui ad alterius non
modo sensum ac voluntatem sed etiam vultum
20 atque nutum convertitur?

Negat quis; nego: ait; aio: postremo imperavi egomet mihi
Omnia assentari :

ut ait idem Terentius, sed ille in Gnathonis persona :
quod amici genus adhibere omnino levitatis est.
25 94. Multi autem Gnathonum similes, cum sint
loco, fortuna, fama superiores, horum est assentatio
molesta, cum ad vanitatem accessit auctoritas.
95. Secerni autem blandus amicus a vero et inter-
nosci tam potest adhibita diligentia, quam omnia
30 fucata et simulata a sinceris atque veris. Contio
quae ex imperitissimis constat, tamen iudicare
solet quid intersit inter popularem, id est, assen-
tatorem et levem civem, et inter constantem et
severum et gravem. 96. Quibus blanditiis C.
35 Papirius nuper influebat in aures contionis, cum
ferret legem de tribunis plebis reficiendis! Dis-

suasimus nos. Sed nihil de me: de Scipione dicam
libentius. Quanta illi, di immortales, fuit gravitas,
quanta in oratione maiestas! ut facile ducem
40 populi Romani, non comitem diceres. Sed adfuistis,
et est in manibus oratio. Itaque lex popularis
suffragiis populi repudiata est.

Atque ut ad me redeam, meministis, Q. Maximo
fratre Scipionis et L. Mancino consulibus quam
45 popularis lex de sacerdotiis C. Licinii Crassi videbatur. Cooptatio enim collegiorum ad populi beneficium transferebatur, atque is primus instituit
in forum versus agere cum populo. Tamen illius
vendibilem orationem religio deorum immortalium
50 nobis defendentibus facile vincebat. Atque id
actum est praetore me, quinquennio ante quam
consul sum factus. Ita re magis quam summa
auctoritate causa illa defensa est.

CHAPTER XXVI

Without sincerity, there can be no loyalty nor true friendship.
Yet flattery harms no one but the flattered who wish not
to be virtuous but only to seem so, and see in flattery a
proof of their virtues.

It is easy to discern the open flatterer: it is the cunning
one against whom we must be on our guard.

97. Quod si in scena, id est, in contione, in qua
rebus fictis et adumbratis loci plurimum est, tamen

verum valet, si modo id patefactum et illustratum
est, quid in amicitia fieri oportet quae tota veritate
perpenditur?   In qua nisi, ut dicitur, apertum pectus 5
videas tuumque ostendas, nihil fidum, nihil ex-
ploratum habeas ; ne amare quidem aut amari,
cum id quam vere fiat ignores. Quamquam ista
assentatio, quamvis perniciosa sit, nocere tamen
nemini potest nisi ei qui eam recipit atque ea delec- 10
tatur. Ita fit ut is assentatoribus patefaciat aures
suas maxime, qui ipse sibi assentetur et se maxime
ipse delectet.

     98. Omnino est amans sui virtus ; optime
enim se ipsa novit quamque amabilis sit intellegit ; 15
ego autem non de virtute nunc loquor, sed de
virtutis opinione.   Virtute enim ipsa non tam multi
praediti esse quam videri volunt. Hos delectat
assentatio ; his fictus ad ipsorum voluntatem
sermo cum adhibetur, orationem illam vanam 20
testimonium esse laudum suarum putant. Nulla
est igitur haec amicitia, cum alter verum audire
non vult, alter ad mentiendum paratus est. Nec
parasitorum in comoediis assentatio faceta nobis
videretur, nisi essent milites gloriosi.   25

          Magnas vero agere gratias Thais mihi?

Satis erat respondere, ' magnas ' ; ' ingentes ', inquit.
Semper auget assentator id quod is, cuius ad

voluntatem dicitur, vult esse magnum. 99. Quam
30 ob rem, quamvis blanda ista vanitas apud eos valet
qui ipsi illam adlectant atque invitant, tamen etiam
graviores constantioresque admonendi sunt ut animum advertant ne callida assentatione capiantur.
Aperte enim adulantem nemo non videt, nişi
35 qui admodum est excors : callidus ille et occultus
ne se insinuet studiose cavendum est. Nec enim
facillime agnoscitur, quippe qui etiam adversando
saepe assentetur, et litigare se simulans blandiatur
atque ad extremum det manus vincique se patiatur,
40 ut is qui illusus sit plus vidisse videatur. Quid
autem turpius quam illudi? Quod ne accidat
cavendum est, ut in Epiclero :

Ut me hodie ante omnes comicos stultos senes
Versaris atque emunxeris lautissime!

45 100. Haec enim etiam in fabulis stultissima persona
est, improvidorum et credulorum senum. Sed nescio
quo pacto ab amicitiis perfectorum hominum, id
est, sapientium, de hac dico sapientia quae videtur
in hominem cadere posse, ad leves amicitias defluxit
50 oratio. Quam ob rem ad illa prima redeamus eaque
ipsa concludamus aliquando.

Chapter XXVII

Recapitulation :

Virtue makes and preserves friendship : the latter is the affection felt for the one who inspires us with love—an affection which should never be sought for advantage, but shared preferably with those of similar age.

So we must ever seek friends, for without friendship, life is joyless.

The essay then concludes with a description of Laelius' friendship with Scipio.

Virtus, virtus, inquam, C. Fanni et tu, Q. Muci, et conciliat amicitias et conservat. In ea est enim convenientia rerum, in ea stabilitas, in ea constantia, quae cum se extulit et ostendit lumen suum et idem
5 adspexit agnovitque in alio, ad id se admovet vicissimque accipit illud quod in altero est, ex quo exardescit sive amor sive amicitia. Utrumque enim dictum est ab amando ; amare autem nihil aliud est nisi eum ipsum diligere quem ames, nulla indigentia,
10 nulla utilitate quaesita ; quae tamen ipsa efflorescit ex amicitia, etiam si tu eam minus secutus sis. 101. Hac nos adulescentes benevolentia senes illos L. Paulum, M. Catonem, C. Gallum, P. Nasicam, Ti. Gracchum Scipionis nostri socerum, dileximus.
15 Haec etiam magis elucet inter aequales ut inter me et Scipionem, L. Furium, P. Rupilium, Sp. Mummium. Vicissim autem senes in adolescentium

caritate acquiescimus, ut in vestra, ut in Q. Tuber-
onis : equidem etiam admodum adulescentis P.
Rutilii, A. Verginii familiaritate delector.   Quoniam- 20
que ita ratio comparata est vitae naturaeque nostrae
ut alia aetas oriatur, maxime quidem optandum
est ut cum aequalibus possis, quibuscum tamquam
e carceribus emissus sis, cum isdem ad calcem,
ut dicitur, pervenire.   25

102. Sed quoniam res humanae fragiles cadu-
caeque sunt, semper aliqui anquirendi sunt quos
diligamus et a quibus diligamur : caritate enim
benevolentiaque sublata omnis est a vita sublata
iucunditas. Mihi quidem Scipio, quamquam est 30
subito ereptus, vivit tamen semperque vivet ;
virtutem enim amavi illius viri quae exstincta
non est. Nec mihi soli versatur ante oculos, qui
illam semper in manibus habui, sed etiam posteris
erit clara et insignis. Nemo unquam animo aut 35
spe maiora suscipiet qui sibi non illius memoriam
atque imaginem proponendam putet.

103. Equidem ex omnibus rebus quas mihi
aut fortuna aut natura tribuit, nihil habeo quod
cum amicitia Scipionis possim comparare. In hac 40
mihi de re publica consensus, in hac rerum privatarum consilium, in eadem requies plena oblecta-
tionis fuit. Nunquam illum ne minima quidem
re offendi quod quidem senserim ; nihil audivi

45 ex eo ipse quod nollem. Una domus erat, idem
victus isque communis ; neque militia solum sed
etiam peregrinationes rusticationesque communes.
104. Nam quid ego de studiis dicam cognoscendi
semper aliquid atque discendi, in quibus remoti
50 ab oculis populi omne otiosum tempus contrivimus?
Quarum rerum recordatio et memoria si una cum
illo occidisset, desiderium coniunctissimi atque
amantissimi viri ferre nullo modo possem. Sed
nec illa exstincta sunt alunturque potius et augen-
55 tur cogitatione et memoria ; et si illis plane orbatus
essem, magnum tamen adfert mihi aetas ipsa
solacium, diutius enim iam in hoc desiderio esse
non possum ; omnia autem brevia tolerabilia esse
debent, etiam si magna sunt. Haec habui de
60 amicitia quae dicerem. Vos autem hortor ut ita
virtutem locetis, sine qua amicitia esse non potest,
ut ea excepta nihil amicitia praestabilius putetis.

NOTES

CHAPTER 1

Line 1. Q. Mucius. Quintus Mucius Scaevola held various magistracies including the consulship (117 B.C.), married a daughter of C. Laelius, and had such a high reputation for his legal knowledge that Cicero was taken by his father to listen to his judgments.

l. 1. augur. The augurs formed a college or guild, said to have been created by Romulus. Their functions—the taking of the auspices to see whether a proposed action had divine approval—were performed as follows : the augur marked out in the heavens with his wand a four-square space of sky called a **templum,** within which he kept observation for a stated time for omens, chiefly thunder and lightning.

l. 2. memoriter et iucunde, 'from memory and in a pleasant manner '.

ll. 2-3. dubitare . . . appellare. Notice that **dubito** followed by the infinitive means ' hesitate '.

l. 3. sapientem. Gaius Laelius was surnamed Sapiens from his skill as a jurist. His famous friendship with Scipio Africanus the younger was the reason why Cicero made him the mouthpiece of this discussion on friendship.

ll. 3-5. ego autem . . . toga, ut, ' on donning the toga virilis I had been introduced by my father to Scaevola, on the condition (ita) that . . . '. A Roman boy wore the toga praetexta (embroidered with purple stripe) until he was about seventeen, when he put on the toga virilis, a plain white woollen garment, the dress of all Roman citizens. The assumption of the toga virilis took place on 17th March, at the feast of Bacchus, whose other name Liber, ' he who frees (from care) ', was regarded as a good omen

67

l. 4. **deductus.** A successful legal career led to high office in the state. Accordingly, Cicero's father placed him with Scaevola, one of the leading jurists of the day. After his death, Cicero went to Scaevola's cousin, the Pontifex Maximus.

ll. 6-7. **multa . . . disputata,** ' many points skilfully discussed ', direct object (with **multa . . . dicta**) of **mandabam.** It was such discussions and pronouncements from experienced jurists that ambitious students like Cicero came to hear.

l. 10. **ad pontificem Scaevolam.** Quintus Mucius Scaevola had a distinguished public career like his cousin the augur, and lost his life in the proscriptions which became a feature of Roman political life in the first century B.C. He was pontifex maximus, i.e. president of the college of priests, who were entirely responsible for the superintendence and maintenance of all religious ceremonies and ritual.

ll. 10-12. **quem . . . dicere,** ' whom I venture to call by far (**unum**) the most eminent in the country both in ability and integrity '.

Note : (i) **unus** with superlatives strengthens and emphasises. (ii) **ingenio, iustitia,** ablatives of respect.

l. 13. **Cum saepe multa, . . . ,** ' I remember that he often not only (discussed) many subjects, but also, sitting at home in his summer-house, as was his custom, when . . . (**cum et . . . familiares**), he chanced upon that topic which just about that time (**tum fere**) was on many persons' lips '.

Note : (i) the necessity to supply **eum dixisse** after **saepe multa,** l. 13. (ii) **cum . . . tum,** ' not only . . . but also '.

l. 17. **Attice.** Atticus, to whom this work on friendship is dedicated, was a great friend of Cicero. A man of great wealth, he nevertheless had no political ambitions and took no part in affairs of state. His fame rests on his close friendship with Cicero and on the frequent letters they exchanged. Atticus preserved those he received from Cicero, and to-day they give us a vivid and intimate picture of Roman life as seen by one who played no small part in the closing years of the Republic.

l. 17. et eo magis, ' and the more so ' ; **eo,** ablative of the measure of difference, found chiefly with comparatives.

l. 18. **P. Sulpicio utebare multum,** ' you were very friendly with P. Sulpicius '.
Note : (i) this meaning of **utor.** (ii) **multum,** an accusative of extent (adverbial accusative) found chiefly with neuter adjectives and pronouns.

l. 18. **tribunus plebis,** ' as tribune of the people '. At this time (first century B.C.) there were ten tribunes annually elected by the votes of the citizens. They exercised wide powers which consisted of : (i) the right to summon the citizens and initiate legislation ; (ii) the right to sit and speak in the Senate ; (iii) the right of veto or obstruction, either to protect individual citizens against arbitrary action on the part of other magistrates or to prevent the passing of bills and proposals in the various assemblies.

Two facts, however, restricted their power : (i) As there were ten tribunes, they could easily be bribed to obstruct one another. (ii) Holding office for one year only, they were unable to put into operation large-scale reforms.

l. 21. **quanta ... querella,** ' how great was the astonishment or regret of men '. This indirect question is the direct object of **meministi,** l. 17.

l. 22. **in eam ipsam mentionem,** ' into mention of that very subject ' : i.e. the fierce quarrel between P. Sulpicius and Q. Pompeius who had been such good friends.

l. 24. **habitum,** perf. partic. pass. in agreement with **sermonem,** best rendered here by a relative clause, ' which had been delivered by him ' (**ab illo**).

l. 25. **C. Fannio, M. F.** Gaius Fannius was a son-in-law of Laelius and son of Marcus Fannius. **M. F. = Marci Filio.**

l. 26. **post mortem Africani.** Africanus (his full name was P. Cornelius Scipio Aemilianus Africanus Minor) was an adopted member of the famous Scipio family. He defeated the Carthaginians in the Third Punic War (146 B.C.), and in 133 successfully brought to an end a campaign in Spain which had caused the Romans much trouble. Shortly after his return from Spain he died in what seemed to be mysterious circumstances. See the note on Chap. XII, l. 13. His friendship with Laelius was proverbial and has been immortalised by Cicero in this treatise on Friendship.

l. 27. **arbitratu meo**, ' in my own way '.

ll. 28-29. **quasi enim . . . interponeretur,** ' for I have introduced them as it were (**quasi**) speaking in person (**ipsos**), to avoid inserting too often " I say " and " he said " ; *lit.* ' lest " I say " and " he said " be inserted too often '.

l. 31. **cum enim . . . ageres,** ' for since you often pleaded with me '. Note this meaning of **ago.**

ll. 32-33. **digna res . . . visa est,** ' the subject seemed worthy '. **cum . . . tum,** ' not only . . . but also '. Note also that **dignus,** ' worthy of ', is followed by the ablative, **cognitione, nostra familiaritate.**

l. 34. **Itaque feci . . . multis,** *lit.* ' and I have done so not unwillingly that I might benefit many '.

l. 35. **ut in Catone Maiore,** ' as in the Cato Major '. Cato the Elder (235–149 B.C.) was a Roman of ' the old school ', upright, honest, stern, and severe. After distinguishing himself in public office and in many military campaigns, he became censor and exercised his ' censorial ' duties with such severity that his name became to later generations a byword for an old-fashioned and unbending morality.

l. 35. **scriptus ad te,** ' dedicated to you '.

ll. 37-38. **quia nulla . . . quam eius qui,** ' because no character seemed more fitted to talk about that time of life than his, since he . . .'*

Note : (i) **quae loqueretur,** consecutive subjunctive (**quae** =**ut ea**) ; similarly **quae . . . dissereret,** l. 43. (ii) **qui . . . fuisset, . . . floruisset. qui** is here causal, =**cum is,** ' since he ', therefore the subjunctive mood is used.

l. 43. **ea ipsa . . . quae disputata,** neuter plurals, accusative case, **ea ipsa** direct object of **dissereret, quae disputata** of **meminisset.**

l. 43. meminisset, subjunctive because it is in a relative clause in oratio or virtual oratio obliqua, dependent on **mihi visa est** (=' I thought ').

ll. 44-45. positum . . . illustrium, ' (when) dependent on the authority of old men and those, (too), famous (ones) '.

l. 46. plus . . . gravitatis. The genitive **gravitatis** (partitive) depends on **plus** and forms the direct object of **habere. nescio quo pacto,** *lit.,* ' I know not in what way ', =' somehow or other '. This phrase is used parenthetically, i.e. without any grammatical influence on the rest of the sentence. Cf. the use of the French *je ne sais quoi.*

l. 47. mea, neuter plural, ' my own work '.

ll. 49-50. senex . . . amicissimus ; these nominatives are in apposition with the pronoun subject of **scripsi,** ' as an old man ', ' as a close friend '.

l. 51. quo, ablative of comparison, ' than whom '.

l. 52. et, ' both '.

l. 53. gloria, ablative with **excellens,** ' in the reputation '.

ll. 54-55. velim . . . avertas . . . putes, ' I should like you to turn . . . (and) to think '. **velim** is a good example of the potential subjunctive *which represents the opinion of the speaker as an opinion.* **avertas, putes** are subjunctives in indirect command, without **ut.**

CHAPTER II

Line 1. Sunt ista, Laeli, ' that is so, Laelius '. Cicero introduces us to the speakers as they are in the middle of a conversation. Note the vocative **Laeli.**

ll. 1-2. nec . . . quisquam, ' nor . . . anyone ' =' and no one '. **Africano,** ablative of comparison.

l. 5. Tribuebatur hoc modo M. Catoni, ' this (name) was recently (**modo**) bestowed on Marcus Cato '.

l. 7. sed uterque alio quodam modo, ' but each (of the two) in a somewhat different way '.

ll. 9-11. **et multa . . . ferebantur,** *lit.* ' and many things of his both in the Senate and in the Forum either wisely foreseen, or firmly done, or shrewdly replied, were reported '; i.e. ' there are many examples related of his wise foresight, firm action, and shrewd replies both in the Senate, etc.'.

ll. 13-15. **Te autem . . . esse sapientem ;** accusative and infinitive dependent on ' men are wont to state ', which can easily be supplied from the following **solent appellare. natura, moribus, studio, doctrina,** ablatives of cause, ' by reason of your natural ability ', etc.

ll. 16-19. **qualem in reliqua Graecia neminem . . . Athenis unum accepimus,** ' such as we have heard no one (was) in the rest of Greece . . . (but) only one man in Athens '.

ll. 17-18. **nam qui septem . . . non habent ; eos** is the antecedent of **qui septem appellantur.** The antecedent of **qui . . . quaerunt** has to be supplied and is the subject of **non habent. septem,** ' the seven wise men ' were Solon of Athens, Thales of Miletus, Pittacus of Mytilene, Bias of Priene, Cleobulus from Rhodes, Myson of Chenae, and Chilon of Sparta. These men, most of whom lived in the sixth century B.C., seem to have made such an impression on their contemporaries and succeeding generations by their prudence and justice that to them were attributed many sayings of worldly wisdom such as, ' Avoid excess ', ' it is hard to be virtuous ', ' know thyself '.

l. 17. **qui ista subtilius quaerunt,** ' (those) who examine those (subjects) somewhat critically '.

l. 19. **eum . . . iudicatum.** The reference is to Socrates, the great Athenian philosopher and teacher, 469–399 B.C. At his trial on a charge of impiety and of corrupting the young, Socrates tells us that he was declared the wisest of men by the Oracle of Apollo at Delphi.

l. 20. **hanc,** ' such '.

l. 21. **omnia tua,** ' all your possessions '.

l. 24. **ex hoc Scaevola,** ' from Scaevola here '.

l. 25. **eoque magis ;** cf. the note on Chap. I, l. **17.**

l. 25. **his proximis Nonis**, ' on the last Nones '. The Nones fall in March, July, October, and May, on the 7th : in the remaining months, on the 5th. The Augurs held a monthly meeting on the Nones to practise their augural art (**commentandi causa**).

l. 26. **in hortos D. Bruti.** Many rich Romans had a **domus** (town house), **villa** (country house and farm), and **horti,** ' suburban estate '.

l. 27. **qui . . . solitus esses,** ' although you had been wont always to observe that day and perform that duty . . . '.
Note: (i) **qui** + subjunctive mood (concessive = ' although '). (ii) **obire** is followed by two objects with slight change of meaning, e.g. **illum diem** (' to observe '), **illud munus** (' to perform ').

l. 32. **cum . . . tum,** ' both . . . and '.

l. 32. **moderate,** ' with composure '.

l. 33. **nec potuisse non commoveri,** ' nor could you not have been moved ', i.e. ' nor could you have remained unmoved '.

l. 33. **nec fuisse id humanitatis tuae,** ' nor was that (characteristic) of your kindliness '. **id,** ' that ', refers to ' the remaining unmoved '.

l. 38. **ab isto officio,** ' from that duty you mention '.

l. 39. **incommodo meo,** ' through any trouble of mine ', ablative of cause.

l. 42. **quod . . . dicis,** ' as to your saying '. **tantum . . . quantum,** correlatives, ' so much . . . as '.

l. 45. **quod quidem magis credo,** ' which I rather think '. Cicero (in the character of Laelius) is referring to the Stoic definition that no one is virtuous except the wise man, the sage, i.e. he who is perfectly acquainted with the truth. The early Stoics, however, admitted no gradations of virtue : hence their ' wise man ', the perfect being, has never existed and is not likely to exist. Thus Laelius is inclined to believe that no one has been ' wise '.

l. 47. **mortem filii tulit.** In this and preceding passages Cicero has admired the stoical endurance of grief. Yet when he himself lost his only daughter about eighteen months before he wrote this essay, he abandoned himself entirely to his sorrow.

l. 48. **hi in pueris,** ' but they (showed fortitude) in the case of children '.

l. 49. **cave anteponas ne istum quidem,** ' beware lest you prefer even him ', i.e. ' don't prefer even him '. **cave, cave ne,** are circumlocutions for the negative imperative (prohibition).

ll. 51-52. **huius . . . illius,** ' of the latter . . . of the former '.

l. 53. **ut . . . loquar,** ' to speak to both of you at once '. (This remark explains the use of the plural **habetote.**)
Note : (i) **utroque** from **uterque,** ' each of two ', ' both '. (ii) **vestrum,** partitive genitive (**vos**).

ll. 52-53. **De me . . . sic habetote,** ' concerning myself . . . take this view '.

CHAPTER III

Line **1. si . . . negem,** ' should I deny '. In conditional sentences of the ideal type, the supposition is more or less fanciful : the present or perfect (for completed action) subjunctive is used in both protasis and apodosis. The apodosis of this sentence is interrupted by the parenthetic clause **quam id . . . sapientes.**

l. 2. **quam . . . sapientes,** ' wise men (i.e. the philosophers) would see how right I am in doing that '. **viderint,** perfect subjunctive (potential). Cf. the note on Chap. I, l. 54.

l. 3. **tali amico . . . qualis,** ' of such a friend . . . as '. Note the correlatives **talis . . . qualis.**

l. 7. **nihil mali,** ' no harm '. The partitive genitive is very common after neuter pronouns and adjectives.

l. 8. **si quid,** ' if any '. Note **quis, quid** ' anyone ', ' anything ', after **si, nisi, num, ne.**

ll. 9-10. **Suis . . . amantis est.** The subject of **est** is **suis incommodis graviter angi,** ' to be greatly distressed at one's own misfortunes '. **amantis,** ' (the characteristic) of one who loves ' ; this participle has **amicum** and **se ipsum** as direct objects.

l. 11. **cum illo . . . praeclare.** Note the phrase **agi praeclare,** ' to go wonderfully well '.

l. 12. **immortalitem,** ' freedom from death '.

l. 15. **de eo iam puero,** ' of him in his childhood '.

l. 17. **factus est consul bis :** i.e. first in 147 B.C., before he was of legal age (**ante tempus**), when in his thirty-eighth year he was a candidate for the aedileship, and again in 134 B.C.

l. 18. **ante tempus, . . . suo tempore,** ' before the (proper) time ' . . . ' at the right time '.

ll. 19-21. **qui . . . delevit.** Translate **eversis** by a present participle, ' by overthrowing ', and take **huic imperio** with **inimicissimis.** The two cities which Scipio destroyed were Carthage (146 B.C.) and Numantia in Central Spain. (133 B.C.)

l. 22. **in matrem,** ' towards his mother '. Similarly **in sorores,** etc.

l. 25. **maerore funeris,** ' by the sorrow shown at his funeral '.

l. 25. **quid,** ' how '.

l. 26. **potuisset,** ' would have been able '. This subjunctive can be explained as conditional (unreal in past time) : the apodosis can easily be supplied from **accessio,** e.g. ' if he had lived any longer '.

l. 28. **ante quam mortuus est.** Note the indicative verb, although it looks as if the sentence is subordinate in an accusative and infinitive construction. Actually the sentence is an addition by Laelius and not part of what he remembered.

l. 29. **eam viriditatem,** ' that freshness '.

l. 32. **vel fortuna, vel gloria,** ablative case, to be taken with **accedere.** The latter is frequently used as the passive of **addo,** ' to be added '.

l. 34. **difficile dictu,** ' difficult to speak '. The ablative of the supine is used chiefly with adjectives (ablative of respect).

l. 34. **quid homines suspicentur,** viz. that he was murdered by Carbo shortly after his return from Spain (129 B.C.). For further details, see Chap. XII. l. 13.

ll. 36-37. **ex multis diebus . . . viderit,** ' of the many glorious and joyful days which he saw in the course of his life '. Note the position of the superlative adjectives, which are *inside* the relative clause and in agreement with the relative pronoun, though in sense they belong to the antecedent, **multis diebus.**

l. 38. **Senatu dimisso,** ' on the adjournment of the senate '.

ll. 38-40. **domum reductus . . Latinis.** Scipio was escorted home by ' allies ' and ' Latins ', because he had that day defended their interest in the matter of public land against the ' commission of three men ' (Triumvirs) who had been appointed by the agrarian law of Tiberius Gracchus to reclaim and distribute in small holdings large tracts of public land. For further details, see the Introduction and the Vocabulary of Proper Names. Allies were united to Rome by treaties, Latins (i.e. those of the Latin status) were incorporated in the Roman commonwealth and possessed the ' private rights ' of citizenship (**ius commercii, ius conubii** [1]) but not the ' public rights ', (**ius suffragii, ius honorum** [2]).

CHAPTER IV

Lines 1-2. **eis qui . . . coeperunt,** i.e. the Epicureans, or followers of the philosophy of Epicurus (342-270 B.C.). He

[1] Right to conduct private suits in the Roman court, and contract a legal marriage.

[2] Right to vote and hold office.

taught that the highest good of man was happiness, i.e.
peace of mind which was to be obtained by leading a
virtuous life. Later followers of his school interpreted
happiness in a different way, i.e. gratification of one's
desires : hence the meaning of the adjective *Epicurean* in
English. Most of the earlier Greek philosophers were
physicists as well, and Epicurus followed the atomistic
doctrines of Democritus, viz. that the universe consisted of
combinations of an infinite number of elementary particles,
atoms. Hence the Epicurean belief that at death, when the
soul and body were severed, the soul ceased to exist, for
its atoms, when deprived of the shelter of the body, were
dispersed owing to their lightness.

l. 6. **quod . . . profecto,** ' which they certainly would not
have done '. This is a good example of a conditional clause,
unreal in past time.

l. 7. **in hac terra,** ' in this land ', i.e. Italy.

l. 8. **magnam Graeciam.** Magna Graecia was the name
given to South Italy and the East portion of Sicily, the
coastline of which was occupied by numerous Greek colonies
sent out from the motherland during the seventh and sixth
centuries B.C. Before the third century B.C. they had had
an independent and interesting existence (**tunc florebat**), but
from 300 B.C. they were gradually absorbed by the growing
power of Rome (**nunc quidem deleta est :** i.e. its freedom
and philosophical schools).

l. 9. **institutis et praeceptis suis erudierunt,** ' by their principles and precepts brought culture to Magna Graecia ',
Laelius is referring to the many schools of philosophy which
flourished in these Greek towns. Greek philosophy had had
its beginnings in the Greek colony of Miletus (Asia Minor)
where it flourished for nearly a century, 600–500 B.C. After
the advance of the Persian Empire to the Aegaean, students
seem to have migrated westwards to the colonies of Magna
Graecia where during the following century, 500–400 B.C.,
many famous schools arose. Perhaps the best known to the
average reader is that of Pythagoras who settled at Croton.

l. 10. vel eius qui . . . iudicatus—another reference to Socrates.

ll. 11-13. qui . . . divinos, ' who did not (say) now this, now that, as (he did) in most cases, but always the same, viz. that the souls of men are divine '.

ll. 14-15. optimoque . . . expeditissimum, ' and for each best and justest the easiest (return) ', i.e. ' and the easiest for the most virtuous and just '. **Quisque** with superlatives and ordinals is loosely equivalent to our ' every ' or ' all '.

l. 16. quod idem Scipioni videbatur, ' which same thing seemed to Scipio ', i.e. ' Scipio held this same view '.

l. 17. quasi praesagiret, ' as if he had a presentiment of his fate '. Note this example of a conditional sentence of comparison : the mood is always subjunctive, the tense depending on the rule of sequence rather than the rule of conditional clauses (ideal and unreal).

l. 22. quae . . . dicebat, ' which he said he had heard through a vision in his sleep from Africanus '. Africanus is Publius Cornelius Scipio Africanus Major. He obtained his title Africanus from his victory over Hannibal at Zama (in Africa) 202 B.C., while Major, ' the Elder ', distinguishes him from his grandson (by adoption), Scipio Africanus Minor, the friend of Laelius. Cicero's dialogue De Republica contains this three days' discussion (purely imaginary of course) and the Dream of Scipio, in which Scipio Africanus Minor is supposed to give the arguments which he had heard in a vision from Scipio Africanus Major.

l. 23. optimi cuiusque animus, ' the souls of all good men '. Cf. the note on l. 14.

ll. 26-27. quocirca . . . amici sit, ' wherefore I fear that to grieve at such a fate as his is (the mark) of an envious man rather than of a friend '. **Maerere** is the subject of **sit**. Note **invidi** and **amici** genitives of possession used as predicates.

l. 28. Sin autem illa veriora ut, ' but if, on the other hand, the truth (is) rather that . . . ' **illa,** as often, refers to what follows.

ll. 29-30. nihil boni . . . nihil mali. Note the partitive genitives, common after neuter pronouns and adjectives denoting amount.

l. 31. fit idem . . . omnino, ' the result is the same as if he had never been born at all '. For quasi, cf. the note on l. 17.

l. 32. quem . . . natum, ' yet that he was born ' : accusative and infinitive dependent on gaudemus and laetabitur.

ll. 34-35. cum illo . . . actum optime est. See the note on Chapter III, l. 11.

l. 36. quem fuerat aequius, ' for whom it would have been fairer '. For the use of the Latin indicative, cf. the use of the indicative with debeo, oportet, possum. Latin expresses *possibility* and *power* as *facts* : we imply *the failure to realise*, e.g. ad mortem te duci oportebat, ' you ought to have been led to execution '.

ll. 39-40. quocum . . . fuit, ' with whom I shared my cares ', etc. Similarly quocum . . . communis.

l. 40. domus et militia, ' the same roof at home and service abroad '.

ll. 43-45. Itaque . . . delectat. Turn into the passive with me as the subject. fama is the antecendent of quam and has dependent on it sapientiae.

l. 45. falsa praesertim, ' especially (as it is) untrue '.

l. 46. Idque mihi eo magis est cordi, ' and that is the (eo) more to the heart to me ', i.e. ' and that is the more welcome to me '. eo, ablative of the measure of difference. cordi, predicative dative with a second dative mihi.

l. 48. vix tria aut quattuor paria amicorum. The four pairs are Theseus and Pirithous, Achilles and Patroclus, Orestes and Pylades, Damon and Pythias.

l. 51. Istuc quidem . . . est, ' that must be so, Laelius '.

ll. 53-55. pergratum mihi feceris, . . . si disputaris (=disputaveris). Both verbs are in the perfect subjunctive and the whole sentence is a good example of an ' ideal ' conditional sentence, ' you would please me very much . . . if you stated . . . '

l. 55. **quid sentias,** ' what you feel ' indirect question. Translate by ' your feelings '.

l. 59. **utrique nostrum,** ' to both of us '. **utrique** is the dative of **uterque.**

CHAPTER V

Line 1. **Ego . . . gravarer, si . . . confiderem**—a good example of a conditional clause, unreal in present time, ' I would not be reluctant (*but I am*), if I had confidence in myself ' (*but I have not*).

l. 2. **res,** ' the subject '.

l. 4. **Doctorum est ista consuetudo,** etc., ' that practice (which you suggest) belongs to philosophers and that too Greeks '.

ll. 5-6. **ut . . . subito,** ' that (a theme) be presented to them which they are to discuss, however suddenly '.

ll. 7-9. **Quam ob rem . . . petatis. quae . . . possunt** is the object of **petatis. censeo (ut) petatis,** ' I think (that) you should seek '.

l. 13. **hoc primum,** ' this first of all '.

l. 14. **neque id ad vivum reseco,** *lit.,* ' nor do I cut it down to the quick ' ; i.e. ' nor do I go into that too deeply '.

l. 15. **ut illi qui . . . disserunt. illi** refers to the Stoics whose definition of the virtuous man is such that it is almost impossible for him to have existed : cf. the note on Chap. II, l. 45. For **subtilius quaerunt,** cf. Chap. II, l. 17.

ll. 15-16. **fortasse vere, . . . parum,** ' perhaps correctly, but not sufficiently (**parum**) in relation to (**ad**) everyday interests '.

l. 19. **mortalis nemo,** ' no mortal man '. **Nemo** often seems to be used as an adjective with nouns denoting persons, but the conception is probably appositional, i.e. ' no one (who is) a mortal '.

ll. 20-21. **non ea quae finguntur aut optantur,** ' not those things which are fancied or hoped for ', i.e. ' not the subjects of our fancies or hopes '.

l. 22. **Nunquam dicam ;** potential subjunctive, ' I would never say '.

ll. 25-26. **sibi habeant ... ; concedant,** jussive subjunctive (i.e. expressing a command in the third person), ' let them keep for themselves . . . let them grant '.

l. 25. **et invidiosum et obscurum,** ' unpopular and unintelligible '.

l. 26. **boni viri,** complement to **fuerint.**

l. 28. **Agamus igitur . . . . Agamus,** iussive subjunctive, ' let us proceed '. **pingui Minerva,** ' with our own poor wit '. Minerva was the goddess of wisdom or intelligence, and the patroness of all the arts and trades. Latin authors frequently use the name of a god or goddess for that which they represent or with which they are associated, e.g. Minerva = ' intelligence ' or ' wit '. **ut aiunt,** ' as they say ', ' as the saying goes ', is the regular expression used to introduce a proverb or well-known maxim.

l. 29. **qui . . . gerunt . . . vivunt,** ' (those) who . . . '.

ll. 30-31. **nec sit in eis ulla cupiditas . . . ,** ' and there is in them no passion ', etc.

l. 31. **sintque magna constantia,** ' and are of great strength of character '. Note the ablative of quality or description, and that it must always consist of noun and adjective.

l. 32. **ut ei fuerunt,** note the indicative mood ; therefore **ut** = ' as ' or ' when ', the former here.

ll. 33-34. **hos . . . putemus,** ' let us consider that these men are worthy-to-be-called (**appellandos**) good men just as they have been accounted so '.

l. 35. **optimam bene vivendi ducem,** ' the best guide to (of) a good life '. Laelius here refers to the Stoic definition of the highest good (**summum bonum**), ' to live in accordance with nature ' (**convenienter naturae vivere**). By this they meant a life of virtue, for they regarded virtue as the law of the universe and the will of God.

l. 37. **mihi perspicere videor,** ' I seem to myself to see ,' i.e. ' it seems that I see '. Latin prefers to use ' seem ' *personally,* English *impersonally.*

ll. 38-39. **societas quaedam, maior . . . accederet,** ' a kind of tie, the stronger as each approaches nearer (to us) '.

l. 42. **satis . . . firmitatis,** ' sufficient (of) constancy '. **firmitatis,** partitive genitive.

l. 42. **hoc,** ablative of respect, ' in this respect '.

ll. 43-46. **quod . . . manet.** Note how clauses (in Latin) are contrasted without a conjunction. The insertion of ' while ' or ' but ' is necessary in English here before **ex amicitia** and **propinquitatis.**

l. 45. **sublata benevolentia,** ablative absolute. This construction may be translated into English in a variety of ways, common ones being adverbial ' when ' and ' after ' clauses. Here, however, a conditional (' if ') clause would be more apt, ' if goodwill is removed (from friendship) '.

l. 45. **nomen,** ' the (very) name '.

l. 49. **res,** ' friendship '.

l. 50. **adducta in angustum,** ' narrowed '.

l. 51. **iungeretur.** Translate this imperfect subj. by the present. The imperfect tense is due to the influence of the perfect tenses (**contracta est et adducta**) on the sequence in the consecutive clause.

CHAPTER VI

Line 2. cum, ' allied with '. In examining this definition of friendship [1] which seems, unnecessarily to us, perhaps, to reject the possibility of friendship between persons whose opinions differ on human and divine matters, we must remember that Laelius is referring to ideal friendship, i.e.

[1] With which compare Chap. IV, ll. 39-43.

the friendship which exists between the good and the wise. And though these latter may not be the ' good and wise men ' of the Stoics, yet they are near enough to that perfection to have complete accord on all subjects both human and divine.

l. 2. **omnium divinarum humanarumque rerum,** objective genitive depending on **consensio.** The name objective is given where the relation of a genitive to the noun on which it depends, is similar to that between an object and its verb.

ll. 3-4. **qua . . . nil melius,** ' than which I do not know whether with the exception of wisdom nothing better ', etc., i.e. ' I am inclined to think that . . . nothing better than this ', etc.

Note : (i) **quā,** ablative of comparison. (ii) **excepta sapientia,** ablative absolute, ' wisdom (having been) excepted '.

l. 8. **extremum,** ' end ', i.e. ' end in life '.

l. 9. **posita,** ' depending '. In the passive, **ponere** frequently means ' to depend (on) '.

l. 14. **interpretemur,** ' let us explain '. Similarly **metiamur** (l. 16), and **numeremus** (l. 17), and **omittamus** (l. 19).

l. 14. **ex consuetudine vitae sermonisque nostri,** ' by the custom of our (everyday) life and speech '.

l. 16. **viros bonos,** ' (as) good men '.

l. 17. **Paulos,** etc., ' men like Paulus, Cato ', etc. Note this use of the plural of these proper names.

l. 18. **his,** ' with men like these '.

l. 19. **eos . . . reperiuntur.** Another reference to the ideally perfect men of the Stoics.

l. 22. **qui,** ' how? ' This form is a survival of what was originally the ablative singular both of the relative and the interrogative pronoun. It occurs also in l. 24 (relative pronoun) and l. 25 (interrogative).

l. 23. **ut ait Ennius.** Ennius (239–169 B.C.) is the greatest figure among the early Roman poets. His principal works

were tragedies and the ' Annales '. The former dealt chiefly
with stories from the Trojan war, while the latter was an
account in hexameters of the history of Rome from its
legendary beginnings down to his own day. Cicero was one
of his admirers and often quotes him.

l. 24. **conquiescat.** Note the subjunctive, consecutive, for
quae =**talis ut ea.** Compare the note on l. 26 below.

l. 24. **quicum,** ' (someone) with whom '. For **qui** (ablative), cf. the note on l. 22.

l. 25. **audeas,** ' you may dare '. The potential subjunctive (i.e. that represents the opinion of the speaker as an
opinion) corresponds roughly to the English ' may ', ' might ',
' must '.

ll. 26-27. **qui . . . gauderet,** ' (someone) to rejoice '. Note
that in Latin an antecedent, if indefinite, is often omitted.
The subjunctive **gauderet** is probably consecutive, for **qui** =
talis ut is, ' of such a kind that he '.

l. 27. **aeque ac tu ipse,** ' as much as you yourself '. **Ac**
(**atque**) is found in comparative sentences with adjectives
and adverbs of *likeness* and *unlikeness,* e.g. **idem . . . ac,**
' same . . . as '; **aliter . . . ac,** ' differently . . . from '.

ll. 28-29. **qui . . . ferret.** For the subjunctive, compare
the note on l. 26.

l. 30. **opportunae sunt singulae rebus fere singulis,** ' are
individually suited to individual things (ends) '.

l. 31. **utare** =**utaris.** Similarly **colare, laudere.**

l. 34. **res,** accusative plural, ' ends '.

l. 34. **verteris,** future perfect. In relative sentences Latin
uses the future and future-perfect with greater exactness
than English.

l. 37. **non aqua, non igni,** ablatives depending on **utimur.**
' Fire ' and ' water ' are proverbially (**ut aiunt**) the prime
necessities of life.

ll. 40-41. **qualis . . . fuit,** ' (such) as was that of the few
who are recorded '.

Note : (i) the necessity to supply **talis as the antecedent of qualis** ; (ii) the incorporation of the adjective **pauci** into the relative clause ; (iii) Laelius' reference to ideal friendship which can exist only between the good and the wise.

l. 42. **partiens communicansque,** ' (by) dividing and sharing it '.

CHAPTER VII

Line 3. **quod . . . in posterum,** ' because it lights up fair hopes for the future '. **bonam spem praelucet,** the accusative is very unusual : perhaps it is best explained as an accusative of the inner object similar to the cognate accusative, **bonam spem** =lumen bonae spei. The term cognate accusative is used when the accusative word is of the same origin as, or of kindred meaning with the verb.

l. 5. **qui intuetur,** ' (he) who gazes upon '.

ll. 7-8. **quod . . . est,** ' what is more difficult to say '. Note the ablative of the supine **dictu,** which is commonly used after adjectives.

l. 9. **amicorum.** This genitive which depends on the three nouns **honos,** ' esteem ', **memoria,** ' remembrance ', and **desiderium,** ' longing ', is subjective. Translate ' (on the part) of friends '.

l. 10. **illorum,** ' the former ', i.e. ' the departed '. **horum,** ' the latter ', i.e. the survivors.

l. 11. **exemeris.** Note the future-perfect. Translate by present. In conditional sentences Latin uses the future and future-perfect with greater exactness than in English. Cf. the note on Chap. VI, l. 34.

l. 14. **Id si minus intellegitur,** ' if that is perceived somewhat little ', i.e. ' if that is not clear '.

ll. 14-15. **quanta . . . sit.** This indirect question depends **on percipi potest.**

ll. 17-18. quae non odiis . . . everti, ' that it cannot be utterly overthrown by animosities and divisions '. quae = ut ea.

l. 19. quantum boni, ' how much good '. Note the partitive genitive.

l. 20. Agrigentinum . . . ferunt. ferunt ' they say '. The reference is to Empedocles, a native of Agrigentum (Sicily). He was born in the first quarter of the fifth century B.C. Like most early philosophers (docti viri), he was interested in physics. His theory, which he expounded in verse (carminibus Graecis), was that four *immutable* elements, earth, air, fire, and water produced the *changing* phenomena of the world as we see it, by association and dissociation. These two actions were produced by Love and Discord respectively.

ll. 21-23. quae . . . moverentur, ' what things in nature and the whole universe are fixed and what things are moved (=are in motion) '.

Note : (i) the relative clause precedes the antecedent. (ii) toto mundo ; with totus, medius, omnis, the ablative of place where is used without a preposition. (iii) The imperfect subjunctive. The historic sequence is due to the influence of the perfect infinitive vaticinatum (esse).

ll. 23-24. ea . . . discordiam. It would be better in translating to turn the verbs into the passive, ' are united by friendship (and) ', etc.

l. 27. quis est qui . . . efferat, ' who is there who does not extol '. Note the subjunctive mood (consecutive), common in relative clauses with an indefinite antecedent. Cf. the note on Chap. VI, l. 26.

l. 28. qui clamores, ' what shouts (were heard) '.

l. 28. tota cavea : for this ablative, cf. the note on l. 21.

l. 29. in nova fabula. This new play of Pacuvius (220–132 B.C.) appears to have had the same subject as Euripides' *Iphigenia in Tauris*. The particular incident which Cicero says was received with such popular enthusiasm, runs as follows : Orestes and his close friend Pylades reach the Tauric Chersonese (the Crimea) to steal the image of the goddess Artemis. Soon after their arrival they are seized by the natives, and, in accordance with the local custom, dragged off to be sacrificed to the goddess. The king, however, allows Pylades to be released. As he does not know which of the two is Orestes (**ignorante rege uter esset Orestes**), Pylades tries to protect Orestes by claiming to be the latter, while Orestes stoutly maintains his own identity.

l. 30. **cum,** conjunction ' when ', to be taken with **diceret . . . perseveraret.**

l. 32. **ita ut erat,** ' as indeed he was '.

l. 33. **stantes :** either ' rising to their feet ' *or* ' the spectators '. The latter meaning is possible because at that time there were no seats in the theatre.

l. 34. **facturos fuisse,** ' would have done '. In indirect statement the future participle and **fuisse** replace the pluperfect subjunctive active of the direct statement (here **fecissent**).

ll. 35-36. **quod . . . non possent.** Note that this relative clause precedes its antecedent **id.**

l. 37. **mihi videor,** ' I think '.

l. 38. **quae ;** this is the neuter plural of the indefinite pronoun **quis,** ' any ', used after **si, nisi, num, ne.**

l. 39. **si videbitur,** ' if it will seem (good to you) ', i.e. ' if you please '.

ll. 39-40. **ab eis . . . qui ista disputant,** i.e. from professional lecturers on philosophy.

l. 41. **Nos . . . potius.** Supply **quaeramus,** ' we would ask '. Note how Cicero relieves Laelius' attempt to define friendship with this interruption : Laelius suggests that he has said all he has got to say, but Fannius and Scaevola press him to continue the discussion. When he does so (in Chap. VIII), he begins to consider the origin of friendship.

l. 43. **sed aliud quoddam filum orationis tuae,** ' but the thread of your discourse is somewhat (**quoddam**) different '. Cicero uses **filum,** ' thread ', metaphorically in the meaning of ' style ' and qualifies the metaphor by **quidam.**

l. 45. **cum . . . disputatum,** ' when there was a discussion on the Republic '. Note **est disputatum,** a good example of an intransitive verb used impersonally in the passive. It is a fairly common construction in Latin and is best translated either personally (' men *or* they discussed ') or by the corresponding noun as in this passage. For the discussion on the Republic, see the note on Chap. IV, l. 22.

l. 47. **accuratam orationem Phili.** In the De Re Publica, Philus maintains the view that no state can be governed without injustice.

l. 50. **Nonne facile ei qui,** ' wouldn't it be easy for one who '.

l. 51. **ceperit :** perfect subjunctive (consecutive). **qui** =**talis ut is,** ' of such a kind that he '.

CHAPTER VIII

Line 1. **Vim hoc . . . adferre,** ' this indeed is to use force '.

l. 3. **in re bona,** ' in a good cause '.

ll. 3-4. **cum . . . tum,** ' not only . . . but also '.

ll. 5-6. **Saepissime . . . solet,** ' very often then to me reflecting on friendship, this is accustomed to seem most worthy of consideration ', i.e. ' as I reflect on friendship, it seems that this ', etc.

ll. 8-10. **ut . . . redderet.** Note that the relative clause, **quod . . . posset,** ' what he can the less (obtain) in himself ', precedes its antecedent **id. dandis recipiendisque meritis,** ' by the giving and receiving of favours '.

l. 12. **et magis a natura ipsa profecta,** ' and more directly derived from nature ' ; *lit.* ' having set out from nature '.

l. 15. **ab eis . . . qui,** ' from those who '.

l. 17. **temporis causa,** ' to suit the occasion ' ; *lit.* ' for the sake of the occasion '.

l. 21. **cum quodam sensu amandi,** " together with a kind of feeling of love '.

ll. 22-23. **cogitatione . . . habitura,** ' by a reflexion how much advantage it would afford '.
Note : (i) **cogitatio,** as a verbal substantive has dependent upon it an indirect question. (ii) **quantum . . . utilitatis,** partitive genitive. (iii) **esset habitura,** periphrastic subjunctive, historic sequence because dependent on the perfect infinitive **orta (esse).**

l. 23. **Quod quidem quale sit : quod** = (' and this ') is the subject of this indirect question.

l. 25. **ex se natos,** ' their offspring ', *lit.* ' (those) born from themselves '.

l. 27. **multo,** ablative of the measure of difference, found chiefly with comparatives.

l. 31. **cuius . . . congruamus,** ' with whose character and disposition we can be in harmony '. **congruamus,** subjunctive in a relative clause expressing purpose.

l. 33. **videamur.** This verb is subjunctive (probably) by attraction after the preceding **congruamus.** The rule for the mood of causal clauses is : (i) indicative for an actual reason of fact ; (ii) subjunctive if subordinate in oratio obliqua *or* virtually subordinate, i.e. when giving an alleged reason (not the speaker's or writer's own).

l. 34. **virtute,** ablative of comparison.

l. 34. **nihil quod . . . adliciat :** for the mood of **adliciat,** cf. the notes on Chap. VII, l. 27, Chap. VI, l. 26.

l. 35. **quippe cum,** ' since '. **cum** = ' since ' is always followed by the subjunctive mood. The causal meaning of **cum** is here strengthened by **quippe.**

ll. 37-38. **Quis est qui . . . usurpet :** for the mood of **usurpet,** cf. the note on Chap. VII, l. 27. Similarly **quis est**

qui non oderit. Remember that the latter verb is perfect in form but present in meaning.

l. 42. **decertatum est** : intransitive verb used impersonally in the passive. Cf. the note on Chap. VII, l. 45. Translate, ' there was a fierce struggle '.

l. 42. **Pyrrho et Hannibale** Pyrrhus, king of Epirus (western Greece), invaded Italy in 280 B.C. at the invitation of the people of Tarentum who were alarmed at the spread of Roman power into Southern Italy. His two victories over the Romans, won at heavy cost, produced no decisive result and Rome's superior man-power eventually compelled him to evacuate the peninsula. The incident to which Cicero refers here as ' upright ' was Pyrrhus' restoration of his Roman prisoners without ransom, in return for the honourable action of the Roman consul Fabricius, who sent to Pyrrhus a traitor who had offered to poison him. Hannibal, the famous Carthaginian general, invaded Italy in 218 B.C., where for the next fifteen years he remained unbeaten in the field. As in the invasion of Pyrrhus, their superior man-power enabled the Romans to hold Hannibal at bay in Italy, and to take the initiative in other fields, e.g. Spain, Sicily and finally Africa itself. In this way they succeeded in securing his recall to Carthage to defend the city. The Romans feared Hannibal as much as Europe did Napoleon ; so perhaps it is not surprising that their historians and writers blackened his character unfairly. There is no historical evidence to show that Hannibal waged war cruelly or treacherously. However, Hannibal in particular and the Carthaginians in general came to be regarded by the Romans as so unscrupulous that **Punica fides** [1] was used to mean ' perfidy '. Cf. the history of the modern expressions ' perfidious Albion ' and ' French leave '.

l. 45. **oderit**, future-perfect = our simple future. Cf. the end of the note on l. 37.

[1] *lit*. Punic (i.e. Carthaginian) faith.

CHAPTER IX

Lines 4-5. quibuscum . . . possunt, *lit.* ' with whom they can be united by intercourse ', i.e. (*more freely*) ' with whom an intimate union is possible '.

l. 7. beneficio accepto . . . adiuncta. These three ablative absolutes may be translated as follows : **beneficio accepto** (*lit.* ' kindness having been received ') = ' by the receipt of kindness ' ; similarly **studio perspecto,** ' affection having been discovered ' = ' by the discovery of affection ' ; while **consuetudine adiuncta** = ' by the addition of intimacy '.

ll. 8-9. quibus rebus . . . adhibitis, ' when these factors are joined ', etc.

l. 11. si qui, ' if any '. Note the indefinite pronoun **quis** (here plural), ' anyone ', ' anything ', used after **si, nisi, num, ne.**

l. 12. ut sit per quem adsequatur, ' so that there be (one) through whom a man may obtain '.
Note : (i) the necessity to supply the antecedent of **per quem.** (ii) **adsequatur,** subjunctive expressing purpose in a relative clause.

l. 14. amicitiae, dative.

l. 14. ex inopia . . . natam, ' born from poverty and want ', i.e. ' the daughter of . . . '.

ll. 16-17. ut . . . arbitraretur, . . . aptissimus, ' in proportion as a man judged there was least (power) in himself, so he would be most fitted for friendship '. **esset,** subjunctive in the apodosis of a conditional sentence, contrary to actual fact in present time. **arbitraretur :** this subjunctive is probably due to the influence of the surrounding conditional sentence.

ll. 18, 19. Ut . . . ut . . . , ' in proportion as '.

l. 20. nullo, the ablative of **nemo,** depending on **egeat.**

l. 21. posita (esse), ' depends (on) '.

l. 21. **in amicitiis . . . colendisque**, ' in friendships to-be-sought and cherished ', i.e. ' in seeking and cherishing friendship '. Note that in the ablative with a preposition, the gerund with an accusative object is replaced by the gerundive construction, i.e. the object takes the case of the gerund and the gerundive is made to agree with it as an adjective.

ll. 23-24. **ne ego quidem illius**, ' nor did I want anything of him either '. Supply **indigens** from l. 23. **ne . . . quidem**, *lit.* ' not . . . even ' = ' nor . . . either '.

l. 24. **ego.** Supply **dilexi** as the verb from **dilexit**, l. 26, and **eum** (=Scipio) as the object.

l. 24. **admiratione quadam**, ablative of cause, ' because of a certain . . . '. **virtutis**, objective genitive, cf. Chap. VI, l. 2.

l. 25. **opinione non nulla**, ablative of cause.

l. 29. **causae diligendi**, ' causes of loving ' = ' causes of our love '.

l. 31. **neque . . . faeneramur**, ' *and* (we) do *not* put out at interest '.

l. 32. **natura**, ablative case.

l. 33. **non spe mercedis adducti.** Translate by a causal clause, ' not because we are ', etc.

l. 36. **Ab his** = ab his sententiis, ' from these opinions '. The subject of **dissentiunt** is the antecedent of **qui** (to be supplied), ' those '.

l. 42. **removeamus, intellegamus.** Cf. **agamus** in Chap. V, l. 28.

l. 43. **sensum diligendi et benevolentiae caritatem**, ' the sentiment of love and feeling of goodwill '.

ll. 43-44. **facta significatione probitatis**, ablative absolute. Translate by a ' when ' clause.

l. 44. **quam qui appetiverunt**, ' those who have longed for it ' (i.e. for moral worth).

ll. 45, 46. **et usu . . . et moribus,** ablative case after **fruantur.**

l. 47. **pares . . . et aequales.** These two adjectives of similar meaning may best be translated by ' fully equal '.

l. 48. **ad bene . . . reposcendum,** ' towards rendering a service than demanding it '. Note **bene mereri,** *lit.* ' to deserve well of ' =' to serve', ' to render service '.

l. 48. **atque,** ' and moreover ', adds a more important to a less important clause.

ll. 50-51. **et erit . . . verior,** ' and its origin, (being derived) from nature (rather) than from weakness, will be both more dignified and real '.

ll. 52-53. **si . . . conglutinaret . . . dissolveret.** Note the imperfect subjunctive (in both protasis and apodosis) in a conditional clause, unreal in present time. ' If advantage cemented friendships (*but it does not*), a change in advantage would dissolve them (*but it does not*) '. **eadem commutata,** *lit.* ' the same (advantage) changed '.

l. 55. **nisi . . . vultis,** ' unless perhaps you wish to make some reply to this '.

l. 58. **minor natu,** ' less in respect of birth ', i.e. ' younger '.

CHAPTER X

The argument thus far may be summarised as follows : Laelius began first by stating that friendship cannot exist except among the good (Chap. V). Then he attempted to define friendship as ' a union on all matters both human and divine, together with goodwill and affection ' (Chap. VI). After describing some of the advantages of friendship and quoting Empedocles' opinion that friendship is that which unites all things in nature and the universe (Chap. VI–VII), Laelius discussed the origin of friendship—natural inclination, and refuted those who support advantage or pleasure as the source of friendship (Chap. VIII–IX). In the rest of the work Laelius discusses the causes which break up friendship, the wrong and right way of employing it, the need for care in the choice of friends, and various rules of behaviour for friends to adopt towards one another.

ll. 5-7. nam . . . sentiretur. The two ut clauses form the subject of the infinitive incidere. The latter is dependent on dicebat, l. 4, *lit.*, ' for it often happened (he said) that the same thing was not expedient or that the same thing was not felt about politics ', i.e. ' that the same course was not expedient or that there was a difference of opinion on politics '.

l. 8. alias . . . alias, ' sometimes . . . sometimes '.

ll. 10-12. quod . . . ponerentur, ' because the strongest attachments of boys were laid aside along with the toga praetexta '.

Note : (i) ponerentur, subjunctive in a causal clause, alleged reason, i.e. ' because, as he said, the strongest ',[1] etc. (ii) una, adverb = together. (iii) toga praetexta, i.e. ' the toga with the purple stripe ' was worn by boys until their sixteenth year when it was replaced by the toga virilis, ' man's toga ', a plain white woollen garment.

l. 12. perducti essent ; the subject is puerorum amores from l. 11 ; so too of dirimi, l. 13.

l. 13. dirimi, infinitive in accusative and infinitive construction—which is continued until the end of the chapter. It will be noticed that *all* the subordinate clauses have their verbs in the subjunctive mood in historic sequence (i.e. imperfect or pluperfect), because the introductory verb dicebat, l. 4, is historic. It will probably be better to translate in direct speech, and change the tenses of subordinate clauses from pluperfect to perfect, imperfect to present, i.e. to the tenses which were actually used by Scipio.

ll. 13-14. contentione vel uxoriae condicionis vel commodi alicuius, ' by rivalry either in courtship (*lit.* a marriage engagement) or for some advantage '. The genitives are objective, for which see the note on Chap. VI, l. 2.

[1] Cf. the note on Chapter VIII, l. 33.

l. 15. **uterque non posset**, ' both cannot '. For the mood of **posset** and the tense of the translation (present for imperfect), see the note on l. 13.

l. 15. **quod si qui**, ' but if any '. **qui** is the plural of **quis, quid**, ' any ', used after **si, nisi, num, ne**.

l. 17. **si . . . incidissent**, ' if they fall into a struggle for office '. **honoris**, another example of the objective genitive. There are more instances in the following lines.

l. 19. **in optimis quibusque**, ' and among the best men '. This use of the superlative adjective with **quisque** is commonly found in the singular, e.g. **optimus quisque**, ' each best man ' = ' the best men '. Perhaps Cicero uses the plural here because he is thinking of pairs of friends.

l. 20. **ex quo . . . exstitisse**. **ex quo = et ex eo**, i.e. the pronoun **quo** is connective rather than relative ; hence the accusative and infinitive is used.

ll. 23-24. **cum . . . postularetur**, ' when something is demanded from friends which is not right '. For the tenses of the translation, see the note on l. 13.

l. 24. **libidinis . . . ad iniuriam**, ' that they be agents in vice or abettors in wrong-doing '.

l. 25. **quod qui recusarent**, ' because (those) who refuse '. The verb of the **quod** clause is **arguerentur**, l. 27. Note that the antecedent of a relative pronoun, if indefinite, has often to be supplied.

l. 26. **ius amicitiae deserere arguerentur**, ' are accused of abandoning the rights of friendship '.

l. 29. **amici causa**, ' for the sake of a friend '. Note **causa**, following its case (genitive) = ' for the sake of '.

l. 30. **eorum querella**, ablative, ' by their complaint '.

ll. 33-34. **ut omnia . . . videri**. Order for translation : **ut diceret subterfugere omnia videri sibi (esse) non modo sapientiae sed etiam felicitatis**. As most of this chapter is in indirect speech (oratio obliqua), it seems unnecessary for Cicero to add **diceret**. We would rather expect **ut**

... **videretur.** (esse) **non** ... **etiam felicitatis,** *lit.* ' to be (a sign) not only of wisdom but also of good luck ' = ' to require not only wisdom but also good luck '.

CHAPTER XI

Line 1. **videamus,** jussive subjunctive, ' let us see '.

ll. 3-4. **Num** ... **ferre** ... **illi** ... **debuerunt,** ' surely ... they ought not to have borne '.

Note : (i) **Num,** introducing a negative question which *expects* the answer ' no '. (ii) **ferre debuerunt,** *lit.* ' they *did ought* to bear '.

l. 3. Coriolanus was a stubborn patrician whose hostility to the election of plebeian magistrates caused his exile. He joined Rome's enemies, the Volsci, and with them advanced on Rome (493 B.C.). His story is told by Livy (II, 33–40) and Plutarch, and forms the subject of one of Shakespeare's Tragedies and one of Beethoven's Overtures.

l. 5. **regnum appetentem,** ' (in) aiming at royal power '. In the early years of the Roman Republic, it was an easy matter for the patricians to get rid of anyone who seemed likely to become too strong or popular in the state, by accusing him of ' aiming at the royal power '. This would be sufficient to alarm the feelings of all sections in Rome with their strong republican bias. Cicero quotes these incidents from early history merely as examples of the point he wishes to make. It is impossible to say whether he was sufficiently interested to examine them critically.

l. 6. **Ti. Gracchum** ... **vexantem,** ' Ti. Gracchus (when he was) disturbing the state '—direct object of **videbamus.** Cicero turns now from the distant past to more recent events. Tiberius Gracchus was tribune in 133 B.C. The date of this imaginary discussion is supposed to be 129 B.C. Actually Cicero was writing in 44 B.C. For Tiberius Gracchus, consult the Introduction. Cicero regarded reformers like Gracchus very much as a staunch conservative might feel towards an extreme left-wing socialist.

l. 10. **ad me qui ... in** consilio, ' to me when I was
helping the consuls Laenas and Rupilius at the enquiry '.
After the murder of Gracchus by the extreme members of
the Senate, the latter appointed a committee of enquiry
which consisted of the consuls for the year, Laenas and
Rupilius, and Laelius. Their task was to punish all those
who had assisted Tiberius.

l. 11. **deprecatum ;** the accusative of the supine is used
to express purpose after verbs of motion, ' to sue for pardon '.

l. 12. **tanti fecisset,** ' he had valued so highly '.
Note : (i) **tanti,** genitive of value or cost ; (ii) **fecisset,**
subjunctive due to virtual oratio obliqua.

l. 13. **quidquid ille vellet sibi faciendum,** ' whatever he
wished was to-be-done by him ', i.e. ' he should do whatever he wished '. The whole clause is, of course, dependent
on **putaret.** Note that in the nominative (and also in the
accusative in oratio obliqua, as here), the gerundive expresses
' ought ', ' must ', ' should '.

ll. 15-16. **voluisset, ... voluisset ... paruissem.** Pluperfect subjunctives in conditional clauses, unreal in past time.
' He would never have wished ', etc.

l. 17. **quam nefaria vox,** ' what a wicked remark '.

l. 19. **Ti. Gracchi temeritati,** dative, depending both on
paruit and **praefuit ;** ' the rashness (i.e. the rash schemes) of
Tib. Gracchus '.

ll. 20-21. **hac amentia,** ablative of cause, ' as a result of
this folly '.

l. 22. **ad hostes,** i.e. to Aristonicus who was trying to seize
the kingdom of Pergamum in Asia Minor which had been
bequeathed to Rome in 133 B.C. After his defeat, Blossius
committed suicide (**poenas ... graves iustasque persolvit**).

l. 24. **peccati,** objective genitive, ' excuse *for* your sin '.

ll. 25-26. **nam ... fuerit,** ' for since the belief in your
virtue was that which united (**conciliatrix**) the friendship '.
Note that **cum =** ' since ' is always followed by the subjunctive mood.

ll. 27-30. **quod si . . . statuerimus . . . simus,** ' now if we should have decided it right, . . . we should be '. Note this conditional sentence, the *ideal* type, where the supposition is more or less fanciful. In the protasis and apodosis the perfect (for complete) and the present subjunctive (for continued action) are used.

l. 29. **perfectā . . . sapientiā,** ablative of quality or description ; ' of faultless wisdom '.

l. 30. **sed loquimur,** etc. In Chap. V, section 18, Laelius says that friendship can exist only among the good, but he rejects the Stoic definition of goodness as a faultless wisdom because, as he says, no mortal has yet attained it. So here, he says they are discussing not perfect friendships but those with which everyday life is familiar (**quos novit vita communis**).

l. 33. **nobis exempla sumenda sunt,** ' examples are to be taken by us ' = ' we must take examples '. The gerundive which in the nominative (and accusative in oratio obliqua) expresses ' ought ', ' must ', ' should ', is *passive*, and used *personally* with transitive verbs, *impersonally* [1] with intransitive verbs. But it is better in translation to turn the construction into the active.

l. 39. **M'** =Manius ; **M.** =Marcus. A Roman had at least two names, the first being his personal name, and the second the name of his gens (clan). Later on a third name became popular, which was given either as an honour to commemorate some victory or merely to denote a branch of the gens. Cf. Gaius Julius Caesar, Marcus Tullius Cicero.

l. 39. **memoriae proditum est,** ' it has been handed down to memory ' = ' it is traditionally remembered '.

l. 41. **quemquam horum,** ' (that) any of them '. Note **quisquam** = ' any ', ' anyone ', after a negative, here **ne . . . quidem,** ' not even '.

l. 43. **esset.** Explain the subjunctive.

[1] i.e. in the neuter.

ll. 43-45. **Nam hoc . . . non fuisse,** order for translation : quid attinet dicere in talibus viris (eum) impetraturum non fuisse hoc quidem, si contendisset. **eum impetraturum non fuisse,** ' that he would not have obtained it', is the oblique form of **impetravisset.**

l. 46. **tale aliquid et facere rogatum et rogare,** ' both to do any such thing (if) asked and to ask it '.

ll. 47-48. **At vero . . . C. Cato.** Laelius means that it was because Carbo and Cato were not as noble as the men he has quoted (Aemilius, etc.), that they were followers of (**sequebantur**) Tiberius Gracchus.

l. 48. **et minime . . . acerrimus,** *lit.* ' and Gaius, his brother (was a follower), then very little, but now most violent(ly) '. Supply **sequebatur** as the verb. Gaius, the younger brother of Tiberius Gracchus, seems to have been on active service with Scipio in Spain during Tiberius' year of office as tribune. Perhaps this explains why he escaped the attentions of the committee of enquiry. However, he was one of the three commissioners chosen to carry out the provisions of Tiberius' agrarian law. On his return to Rome he probably lay low and avoided public affairs, but by 129 B.C. (the date of this dialogue) Laelius suggests that Gaius was taking an active part in politics, no doubt as leader of the survivors of his brother's supporters. He was not elected tribune, however, until 123 B.C.

CHAPTER XII

Line 1. **sanciatur.** Note the subjunctive mood (iussive) ; ' let this law be established '.

l. 3. **minime accipienda,** ' least to-be-received ' = ' by no means to be admitted '.

l. 4. **cum . . . tum,** ' not only . . . but also '.

l. 6. **eo loco,** ' in such a position ', i.e. from a political point of view.

l. 6. Fanni, vocative of Fannius.

ll. 8-9. Deflexit . . . maiorum, ' the political practice of our ancestors has already swerved far from its track and course '. **spatio curriculoque,** the metaphor is taken from the racecourse. These remarks are more applicable to Cicero's own day than to 129 B.C., the date of this dialogue. Cicero wrote in 44 B.C., and the period between 129 and 44 B.C. saw the gradual collapse of the republican constitution and its failure to maintain order, security and decent government. Cicero, as a staunch conservative, attributes this collapse to the mischievous activities of men like Tiberius Gracchus. The real reason, however, was the refusal of the senate to put its own house in order and move with the times.

l. 10. vel . . . paucos menses, ' or rather he actually did reign for a few months '. **is quidem.** The demonstrative pronouns are frequently strengthened by **quidem.** The Romans were somewhat like the modern Americans in their attitude to being governed by kings. Thus Cicero makes Laelius accuse Tiberius of holding almost a royal position with absolute power in the Roman Republic. For a time, early in 133 B.C., after Tiberius had succeeded in deposing one of his colleagues whom the Senate had pressed to obstruct him, he possessed a power which was greater than that of other magistrates. It was, however, by no means absolute, for: (i) he was elected by the free vote of a popular assembly, (ii) he held office for one year only.

l. 11. Num, ' surely . . . not ', introduces a negative question which expects the answer ' no '.

l. 11. quid simile, ' anything like (it) '.

ll. 12-14. Hunc . . . non queo dicere. Order for translation : **non queo dicere sine lacrimis quid amici et propinqui secuti hunc etiam post mortem effecerint in P. Scipione.**

l. 13. in P. Scipione, ' in the case of P. Scipio '. Publius Scipio had already incurred the hostility of Gracchus' supporters and the mob in 131 when he opposed Carbo's measure to make the re-election of tribunes legal. Again in 129 B.C. he came into collision with this party by proposing that the decision of disputes concerning land belonging to the Italian allies should be removed from the three Land Commissioners. Thus there were frequent quarrels in the Forum. After being conducted home one evening by members of the Senate and prominent Italian allies, the next day Scipio was found dead in his bed. There were many rumours of foul play, and Cicero seems to believe that Gracchus' supporters, especially Carbo, were responsible. Two facts suggest, however, that death was due to natural causes : (i) no enquiry was held, (ii) the surprising failure of Scipio's friends to secure a conviction (i.e. assuming that Scipio had been murdered).

l. 15. **Carbonem,** direct object of **sustinuimus.** Carbo, a person of little principle but great oratorical power,[1] first came to the front when he was chosen by C. Gracchus to fill a vacancy in the Land Commission. During his tribunate in 131 B.C. he made an important proposal that tribunes should be eligible for annual re-election ; in other words, Carbo was trying to remove from the tribunate its chief weakness, namely, the limited tenure of office. The Senate met the challenge and Scipio, using all his efforts, was successful in quashing it. See also the preceding note.

l. 15. **propter recentem poenam Ti. Gracchi,** ' on account of the recent punishment of Ti. Gracchus '. Laelius means that the Senatorial party had to go carefully, because the murder of Tiberius Gracchus was too recent to have been forgotten by the people of Rome. Hence they had ' to put up with ' Carbo, although they would, no doubt, have liked to have taken much stronger measures.

l. 17. **non libet augurari,** ' I am not minded to prophesy ', with dependent question **quid . . . exspectem. non libet** (supply **mihi**), ' it does not please me '.

l. 18. **res,** ' trouble ', ' revolution '.

---

[1] *Cambridge Ancient History,* Vol. **IX**, p. 38.

l. 19. **cum semel coepit** (supply labi), ' when once it has begun to fall '.

l. 19. **in tabella**, ' in the matter of the ballot '. Up to this time, votes in the elections of the various magistracies had been given *viva voce*. In 139 B.C. Gabinius passed a bill which introduced the ballot at elections. Two years later this provision was extended to voting on judicial issues [1] by a law of Cassius (**lege Cassia**). In 131 B.C. Carbo extended the use of the ballot to legislation. The point of all this is that the poorer voters, many of whom were dependent on their richer fellow-citizens, could now exercise their right to vote without fear of victimisation. Laelius' reaction to these important reforms is typical of the senatorial order of those days. This obstinate refusal to see any good in those who did not belong to or support the governing class, coupled with a firm determination to retain all the fruits of office within their own circle was chiefly responsible for the eventual collapse of the Roman Republic.

l. 26. **Praecipiendum est bonis**, ' it is to-be-enforced on the good ' = ' it must be enforced '. Note that in the nominative the gerundive (+parts of the verb **esse**) expresses ' ought ', ' must ', ' should '. **boni**, ' good men ' is used here in a political, not a moral meaning. Hence it refers to members of the senatorial party.

l. 29. **in magna aliqua re publica peccantibus**, ' (when they) do wrong in an important matter concerning the state '.

l. 33. **Themistocle**, ' than Themistocles ', ablative of comparison.

l. 34. **bello Persico.** The most famous battles of this, the third Persian invasion of Greece, were Thermopylae (480 B.C.), where the Spartans made their famous stand, Salamis (480 B.C.), where the Greek fleet inflicted a crushing defeat on the Persian squadrons, and Plataea (479 B.C.), in which the Greek land forces decisively defeated the Persian

[1] Except in cases of high treason.

infantry. It was in connection with the sea fight off Salamis that Themistocles ' delivered Greece from slavery '.

l. 35. **propter invidiam.** Themistocles' exile in 471 B.C. may have been due to financial corruption which gave his conservative opponents an opportunity to get rid of him. While in exile he incurred the suspicions of both Athens and Sparta by corresponding with Pausanias, the Spartan king, who at this time was conducting a treasonable correspondence with Persia. Fleeing to Persia, he was hospitably received and given an allowance by the Persian king. It is doubtful whether there is any truth in the rumours that he offered to betray Greece to Artaxerxes, the Persian king.

l. 36. **non tulit,** ' he did not endure '.

l. 39. **itaque mortem,** etc. The belief that Themistocles committed suicide by drinking bull's blood may have arisen from the misunderstanding of a statue which was erected by the natives of Magnesia, of which Themistocles had been appointed governor by the Persian king. This piece of sculpture represented the Athenian pouring bull's blood over an altar. Actually Thucydides, our best authority, says that he died a natural death. Of Coriolanus' death there are two versions, one that he lived to an old age (Pictor in Livy, II, 40), and secondly that he was killed by the Volscians in revenge for his sparing Rome (Plutarch).

l. 41. **excusatione amicitiae,** ' by the plea of friendship '. **amicitiae,** objective genitive.

ll. 42-43. **ut ne quis concessum putet,** ' that no one may think it permissible '.

Note : (i) **ut ne** for the more usual **ne** ; (ii) **ne quis,** ' that no one '.

ll. 44-45. **Quod . . . haud scio an aliquando futurum sit,** ' which I know not whether will one day happen ', i.e. ' and this will probably one day happen '. Note **haud scio an,** ' I know not whether ' = ' perhaps ', ' probably '. **quod,** ' and this ', i.e. the possibility of a man invading his native country. This actually happened in the first century B.C.

when Caesar invaded Italy in 51 B.C. at the outbreak of civil war between himself and Pompey, the leader of the senatorial party. Cicero makes Laelius speak prophetically of what really happened.

ll. 45-46. **Mihi . . . curae est,** ' it is (for) no less a care to me ', i.e. ' I am no less concerned '.

CHAPTER XIII

Line 3. **ne exspectemus quidem,** ' let us not even wait '. The following subjunctives, **adsit, absit,** etc., similarly express *commands* (iussive subjunctive).

l. 3. **dum rogemur,** ' until we are asked '. **dum** (=' until ') follows the rule of other temporal conjunctions, i.e. if strictly temporal, it is followed by the indicative mood ; but if some other idea than that of time (prospective *as here*, anticipation, purpose, prevention, etc.) occurs, it is followed by the subjunctive mood.

l., 6. **amicorum bene suadentium,** ' of friends who give wise advice '.

l. 9. **et adhibitae pareatur,** *lit.* ' and let there be obedience to (it) (when) used ', i.e. ' and let it be obeyed when used '. **adhibitae** is dative, in agreement with **ei** = **auctoritati** (understood). Note that **pareo,** being an intransitive verb, can be used only impersonally in the passive.

ll. 9-11. **Nam . . . quaedam :** order for translation, **nam opinor quaedam mirabilia placuisse quibusdam quos audio,** etc. **audio** =' I am told '. **placuisse,** ' have pleased ' = ' have found favour with '. It is not certain to what sages Cicero is referring.

l. 12. **partim fugiendas,** etc., the following accusative and infinitives detail these ' astonishing opinions ' (**mirabilia quaedam**).

l. 12. **fugiendas esse nimias amicitias,** ' that excessive friendships are to-be-avoided ' = ' should be avoided '.

ll. **14-15. satis . . . rerum**, ' that there is sufficient and
more to each man of his own affairs ', i.e. ' that every man
has enough and to spare of his own business '.

l. **15. alienis,** supply **rebus,** i.e. ' in the affairs of others '.

l. **17. quas . . . adducas . . . remittas.** Note the subjunctives expressing purpose. The relative pronoun **quas** =**ut
eas.**

l. **18. ad beate vivendum,** ' for living happily ' =' for a
happy life '. Epicurus (341–270 B.C.) taught that pleasure
or absence from pain is the only good. Elsewhere (1 N. D.
20, 53), Cicero gives Epicurus' definition of happiness as
' harmony of the soul and freedom from every tie '. See
also the note on Chap. IV, l. 1.

l. **21. Alios.** Laelius here refers to the later followers
either of Epicurus or of Aristippus. The latter, who may be
regarded as the forerunner of Epicurus, regarded pleasure
as the only absolute good in life.

l. **21. multo etiam inhumanius,** ' much more heartlessly ',
to be taken with **dicere.** Note **multo,** ablative of the
measure of difference ; similarly **paulo,** l. 22.

l. **22. quem locum,** ' a topic which '.

l. **22. paulo ante,** i.e. in Chap. VIII, ll. 7 ff.

l. **25. itaque ut quisque,** etc., ' and so (in proportion) as
each man has least (of) firmness and least (of) strength, so
he longs for friendship most '.

l. **30. O praeclaram sapientiam,** accusative of exclamation, ' O noble philosophy '.

l. **31. videntur.** The subject is **ei,** ' those ', the unexpressed antecedent of **qui . . . tollunt.**

l. **31. qua,** ablative of comparison, ' than which '.

l. **37. aut susceptam deponere,** ' or to lay aside (when
once) taken up '. The object of both infinitives is **ullam
honestam rem.**

ll. **38-39. quae necesse est cum aliqua cura . . . aspernetur
atque oderit,** *lit.* ' which, it is necessary with some trouble

rejects and hates '. The emphasis seems to lie on **cum aliqua cura** : thus we may translate : ' which must meet with some trouble in rejecting and hating '.

l. 43. **animi bene constituti,** ' of a well regulated mind '.

l. 46. **qui profecto cadit,** ' as it certainly does befall '.

l. 49. **ne . . . suscipiamus,** ' in order that we may not incur ', i.e. ' to avoid incurring '.

l. 50. **motu animi sublato,** ' when emotion in the soul is removed '. **sublatus,** perfect participle passive of **tollo.**

l. 53. **Neque enim sunt isti audiendi,** ' nor indeed are those to be listened to ', i.e. ' nor should we listen to those '. **isti,** the Stoics, for whom see Chap. II, l. 45.

l. 55. **cum . . . tum,** ' not only . . . but also '.

ll. 56-57. **ut . . . contrahatur,** ' that it expands, so to speak, at the good (fortune) of a friend and contracts with his adversity '. The metaphor is probably taken from the reaction of liquid to heat and cold.

l. 59. **non tantum valet,** ' is not so strong '. **tantum,** accusative of extent, found chiefly with neuter adjectives and pronouns.

l. 60. **non plus quam,** ' any more than '.

CHAPTER XIV

Lines 1-2. **cum . . . eluceat.** The subject of **contrahat** is the sentence **si qua . . . eluceat,** *lit.* ' if any evidence of virtue should shine forth '. Translate it by ' the evidence of shining virtue '. Note: **cum =** ' since ' is always followed by the subjunctive mood.

l. 1. **ut supra dixi,** i.e. in Chap. IX.

l. 3. **ad quam . . . applicet et adiungat.** Note the sub-junctive mood in the relative clause. It expresses purpose.

l. 6. **cultuque corporis,** ' and personal adornment '.

ll. 7-9. **animante . . . delectari.** Supply ' and yet ' before this phrase which is contrasted with the preceding **delectari**

. . . corporis. This omission of a conjunction when clauses or phrases are contrasted is very characteristic of Latin. It is called asyndeton. The order for translation is **non admodum delectari animante praedito virtute, eo qui,** etc.

ll. 7-8. **eo qui . . . possit,** ' in one who can ', etc. Note the subjunctive mood **possit,** consecutive for **qui** = talis ut is, ' of such a kind that '.

ll. 9, 10. **remuneratione . . . vicissitudine,** ablatives of comparison after **iucundius.**

l. 14. **quam ad amicitiam similitudo,** ' as likeness (does) to friendship '.

ll. 14-15. **verum esse ut,** ' that it is true that '.

ll. 15-16. **quasi . . . natura,** ' united, so to speak, in relationship and nature ', i.e. ' in a natural relationship '.

l. 17. **similium sui,** ' for things like itself ', objective genitive, dependent on **appetentius** and **rapacius.** For an explanation of this genitive, see the note on Chap. VI, l. 2.

ll. 19-20. **bonis . . . benevolentiam.** Supply **esse,** ' that there is ', etc.

l. 21. **qui . . . fons.** The relative pronoun, which, strictly speaking, should agree in gender with the antecedent **benevolentiam,** is attracted into the gender of the complement **fons.**

ll. 22-25. **Non est enim . . . quae . . . soleat,** ' for it (i.e. goodness, **bonitas**) is no unfeeling, selfish or proud virtue, inasmuch as it is wont '. Note **quae** = cum ea, ' since it ' : hence the subjunctive mood **soleat.**

ll. 25-26. **quod non faceret . . . si . . . abhorreret,** ' which it would not do . . . , if it shrank '. This is a good example of a conditional sentence *unreal* in *present* time : note the *imperfect* subjunctive in both protasis and apodosis.

l. 27. **qui . . . ,** ' those who, etc.'. Laelius is referring to those whose opinions he gives in Chap. XIII, ll. 23-24.

l. 30. **parta,** perfect participle passive of **pario.**

l. 31. **tum . . . ,** to be taken closely with the following **si ;** translate by ' only '.

ll. 34-36. **ut ei qui . . . beneficentissimi ;** order for translation : **ut ei qui, praediti** (being endowed) **opibus et copiis maximeque virtute in qua . . . praesidii, indigeant alterius minime, sint liberalissimi et beneficentissimi.**

l. 35. **alterius,** supply ' help ' as the object of **indigeant.**

l. 35. **plurimum praesidii,** ' most (of) protection '. Note the partitive genitive. As Shuckburgh remarks, Cicero's argument here is not very convincing. We are not likely to be persuaded that friendship is not cultivated for advantage merely by the fact that the wealthiest, even if also the most virtuous, are very generous and kind. Cicero's line of argument, however, seems to be as follows : the wealthiest men have little need of anyone, so, if friendship is formed merely for advantage, they above all others have no need of friendship ; yet they are most generous and kind, apparently to retain their friends. Thus the need for friendship is not based on the need for advantage or gain.

ll. 37-38. **Atque haud . . . amicis,** *lit.* ' and moreover I do not know whether it is not even expedient that nothing ever at all be lacking to friends '. For **haud scio an** = ' perhaps ', ' probably ', see Chap. XII, l. 45. We may translate as follows : ' perhaps it is not even expedient that friends should never lack anything at all '.

l. 38. **ubi,** ' how '.

l. 39. **viguissent, si . . . eguisset :** conditional sentence *unreal* in *past* time. ' How would my affection have been displayed if ', etc. In Chap. IX, l. 22, however, Laelius states that Scipio had no need of him ; **Quid enim? Africanus indigens mei? Minime hercle.**

CHAPTER XV

Line 1. **non ergo erunt homines . . . audiendi,** ' men . . . will not therefore have to be listened to ', i.e. ' we shall not have, then, to listen to men . . . '.

l. 1. **deliciis diffluentes,** ' abandoned to luxury '. **diffluere** literally means ' to flow away '. The idea seems to be of a person dissipating his strength in luxury.

l. 4. **pro deorum fidem atque hominum,** ' by the faith of gods and men '. **pro** is here an interjection, O! Ah! Alas! and **fidem** is an accusative of exclamation. See also Chap. XIII, l. 30.

ll. 3-4. **Nam quis est . . . qui velit,** ' for who is there who would wish '. **velit** is here a consecutive subjunctive, for **qui** = **talis ut is,** ' of such a kind that he '.

l. 5. **ut,** ' on condition that '.

l. 8. **nimirum,** ' forsooth ', here ironically.

l. 10. **omnia semper . . . sollicita,** ' everywhere is suspicion and anxiety '.

ll. 11-12. **Quis enim . . . metuat,** ' for who would love either the man whom he fears '. **metuat,** the subjunctive is due to attraction.

l. 13. **Coluntur.** The subject is ' tyrants '.

l. 13. **dumtaxat ad tempus,** ' merely for a time '.

l. 14. **ceciderint,** future-perfect. Translate by present. Note that Latin is more precise in its use of tenses, particularly in conditional, temporal and relative clauses.

l. 15. **fuerint,** perfect subjunctive, in indirect question.

l. 15. **Quod,** ' and this ', direct object of **intellexisse.**

l. 16. **ferunt,** ' they say '. The order for translation in this sentence is as follows : **quod ferunt Tarquinium dixisse exsulantem—se intellexisse,** etc.

l. 16. **tum,** to be taken closely with **cum,** l. 18, ' only when '.

l. 19. **miror . . . si,** ' I wonder that '.

l. 19. **illa superbia et importunitate,** ' considering his well-known (illa) pride and insolence '. This ablative is that of quality or description.

l. 26. **nec quicquam,** ' and nothing '.

l. 26. **insipiente fortunato,** ablative of comparison.

ll. 27-28. **Atque hoc quidem videre licet,** 'and this you may see that', etc.

l. 28. **commodis moribus,** ' of affable character ', ablative of description or quality, which always consist of noun and adjective.

l. 30. **sperni . . . novis,** the subject of **sperni** is **amicitias,** while **indulgeri** is an example of an intransitive verb used *impersonally* in the passive. Translate it as though it were in the active, with ' they ' as subject.

l. 33. **parare,** ' to acquire '.

l. 34. **amicos non parare,** ' (and) not to acquire friends '. For the asyndeton, see the note on Chap. XIV, ll. 7-9.

l. 35. **ut ita dicam,** ' so to speak '. In this way Cicero introduces the metaphor of calling friends ' the fairest furniture of life '. In many other passages he uses **quidam, quasi,** and **ut aiunt** in a similar way.

ll. 37-38. **eius enim . . . viribus,** *lit.* ' for each one of those things is of him who has conquered by his strength ', i.e. ' for everyone of those things belongs to the strongest '.

ll. 38-39. **amicitiarum . . . possessio ;** order for translation : **sua possessio amicitiarum permanet cuique stabilis et certa.**

l. 42. **haec hactenus,** *lit.* ' these things no farther ', i.e. ' so much for this '.

CHAPTER XVI

Line 1. **Constituendi autem sunt ;** translate personally and in the active, ' now we have to determine '.

l. 2. **diligendi,** ' of loving ' =' of affection '.

l. 4. **eodem modo . . . quo,** ' in the same way . . . as '.

l. 5. **in amicos,** ' towards our friends '.

l. 6. **illorum erga nos benevolentiae. benevolentiae** is dative, depending on **respondeat.**

ll. 7-8. ut quanti . . . amicis, ' that as a man values himself, so he should be valued by his friends '. Note the correlatives **quanti . . . tanti,** genitives of price, *lit.,* ' at what value . . . at such a value '.

l. 9. nulli, dative case after **assentior.**

l. 10. quem ad modum in se quisque ; supply **sit animatus.**

l. 12. nostra causa, ablative case, ' for our own sakes '. Cf. **causa amicorum,** ' for our friends' sake '.

l. 14. tum, ' again '.

ll. 14, 15. acerbius . . . vehementius, comparative adverbs, ' too bitterly . . . too strongly '.

ll. 15-16. quae . . . honestissime, ' (actions) which are not quite honourable in our own affairs, become very much so **(honestissime)** (if) on behalf of our friends '. **in amicorum,** supply **rebus.**

l. 17. res, ' occasions '.

ll. 20-21. paribus officiis ac voluntatibus, ' to an equal (interchange of) kind offices and feelings '.

ll. 21-22. Hoc . . . amicitiam, ' this is to call friendship to a too mean and petty reckoning '. **exigue** and **exiliter** are actually adverbs, but it will improve our translation if we take them with the noun **calculos.**

ll. 26–28. ne . . . congeratur, ' that some (kindness) overflow or spill to the ground, or that more than is right be heaped upon friendship '. **plus aequo,** note the ablative of comparison. Laelius seems to be thinking of friendship in terms of a basket or bin into which kind acts are heaped. He means that there is no fear that these kind offices, if abundantly and profusely bestowed, will overflow and spill on to the ground and so be lost.

l. 29. quanti . . . tanti, see the note on l. 7 above.

ll. 31-32. abiectior . . . fractior. For the translation of the comparatives, see the note on ll. 14, 15.

ll. 32-33. Non est igitur amici . . . in se est, ' therefore it is not (the duty) of a friend to be such towards another (eum) as the latter is towards himself '. For **talem esse in eum qualis**, etc., we might say, ' to have the same opinion of another as the latter has ', etc. **amici**, for this genitive, cf. Chap. X, l. 33.

l. 34. **eniti et efficere ut**, ' to strive and bring about that ' =' to strive to bring about that '.

l. 35. **spem cogitationemque meliorem**, ' better hope and thought ' =' hopes and thoughts of better things '.

ll. 37-38. **si prius . . . dixero**, ' if I first shall have said ' =' after I have first said '.

l. 39. **quam eius qui**, ' than his who '.

l. 40. **ita amare oportere ut si**, ' that we ought so to love as if '.

l. 42. **a Biante**. Bias (*c.* 550 B.C.) was a native of Priene in Ionia (Asia Minor), and included by the Greeks among their seven wise men. The sayings which are attributed to them are usually full of shrewdness and common sense, but the maxim attributed to Bias in the text is somewhat cynical. Other sayings of a similar character are : ' most men are bad ' ; ' of the gods say only that they are gods '.

ll. 43-45. **impuri . . . sententiam**, ' (he said that) it was the opinion of some sordid or selfish (fellow) or of one who regarded everything in relation to (**ad**) his own power '.

l. 48. **quo plures det . . .**, note that when a purpose clause contains a comparative, **ut** is replaced by **quo**.

l. 49. **tamquam ansas ad reprehendendum**, ' handles, so to speak, to take hold of ', i.e. opportunities for criticism and censure.

l. 50. **recte factis commodisque amicorum**, ' at the good deeds and success of his friends '.

l. 53. **Illud potius praecipiendum fuit**, ' the following (illud) was rather to-be-enjoined ' =' should rather have been enjoined '.

l. 55. **ut ne quando . . . inciperemus**, ' that we should not at any time begin '. For **ut ne =ne**, cf. Chap. XII, l. 42.

l. 57. **in deligendo,** ' in choosing (a friend) ', i.e. ' in our choice of a friend '.

ll. 57-59. **ferendum id Scipio . . . putabat,** ' Scipio thought that it was to-be-borne rather than the time of a breach be-devised '. Translate the gerundives *personally*, i.e. ' that we should bear it rather than ', etc.

CHAPTER XVII

Line 1. **utendum,** ' that we should adopt '. For the translation, see the preceding note.

l. 1. **ut,** ' namely that '.

l. 4. **ut etiam.** This sentence introduces a limitation to the general limit given in ll. 1-4.

l. 4. **si qua fortuna,** ' if any chance '. **qua** is the feminine of the indefinite adjective, **qui, quae (qua), quod,** ' some ', ' any '. This, as also the indefinite pronoun **quis, qua, quid,** is used after **si, nisi, num, ne.**

l. 5. **minus iustae,** ' less honourable ' =' somewhat dishonourable '.

ll. 6-7. **in quibus . . . fama,** ' in which their life or reputation is at stake '. Note this meaning of the passive of **ago,** ' to be at stake '. **caput** may possibly mean here ' civil status '.

l. 7. **declinandum sit de via,** ' we should deviate from the (straight) path '. For the translation of the gerundive, see the note on l. 1 and on Chap. XVI, l. 57.

l. 7. **modo,** ' provided that '. Note the negative **ne** and the subjunctive mood **sequatur.**

ll. 8-9. **est enim quatenus . . . possit,** ' for there is a to-which-extent . . . ', i.e. ' there is a certain extent to which . . . '.

ll. 10-12. **nec mediocre . . . turpe est :** order for translation, **oportet existimare benevolentiam civium, quam . . . turpe est, nec (=no) mediocre telum ad res gerendas.**

l. 10. **ad res gerendas,** ' for things to-be-done ' =' for doing things ' =' in our actions '.

l. 16. **omnibus in rebus,** ' in everything else (but friend-ship) '.

l. 17. **capras . . . posse,** the subject of **dicere posse** is **quisque,** ' a man ', in the dependent question **quot quisque haberet.**

l. 18. **amicos . . . dicere ;** supply ' and yet ' before this clause. For the asyndeton, see the note on Chap. XIV, ll. 7-9.

l. 19. **in illis quidem parandis,** ' in them to-be-acquired ' =' in acquiring them '. Note this gerundive construction which in Latin is found in the accusative, dative and ablative with a preposition, where in English the gerund governing a direct object is used. Cf. **ad res gerendas** of l. 10 above and **in amicis eligendis** of the next line. Scipio is surprised that we do not use some method of testing the fitness of acquaintances to be our friends, just as men look for those signs and marks which in cattle and animals reveal their soundness and quality.

ll. 21-22. **quibus eos . . . iudicarent,** ' by which to judge those '. The subjunctive expresses purpose.

l. 24. **sane nisi expertum,** ' unless you have actually tried a man '. **expertum** is accusative case in agreement with the unexpressed subject of **iudicare.**

l. 26. **experiendi,** ' of trying ' =' of trial '.

ll. 27-30. **Est igitur prudentis . . . amicorum,** ' it is there-fore (the part) of a wise man to check the impetus of good-will just as (he would) his course, in order that we may adopt a friendship when the character of our friends has been to some extent (**ex aliqua parte**) tested, just as (**quasi**) (we would use) horses (only after they have been) tried '. For the genitive **prudentis,** see Chap. X, l. 33. **periclitatus,** the perfect participle of the deponent verb **periclitor,** is here used in a passive sense. **amicitia** (so also **equis temptatis**) is ablative after **utamur.**

l. 30. in parva pecunia, ' in small (sums of) money '.

ll. 33-34. qui . . . sordidum existiment, ' to think it mean '. **existiment,** consecutive subjunctive, for **qui =tales ut ei,** ' of such a kind that they '.

l. 35. magistratus, imperia, ' civil and military positions '.

l. 36. anteponant. See the preceding note.

ll. 36, 37. ex altera parte . . . ex altera, ' on the one hand . . . on the other '.

l. 38. multo, ' by much ' =' much ' ; ablative of the measure of difference, which is used here owing to the comparative idea contained in **malint.**

l. 38. illa, ' the former '.

l. 39. ad contemnendam potentiam. See the note on l. 19 above.

ll. 39-40. quam . . . arbitrantur. quam is the direct object of **consecuti sunt ;** translate by ' it '. **neglecta amicitia,** ablative absolute, ' friendship neglected ' =' by the neglect of friendship '. **obscuratum iri,** ' that (the crime) will be forgotten '. The ' crime ' is the neglect of friendship.

l. 44. qui . . . anteponat. For the subjunctive, see the note on ll. 33-34 above.

ll. 46-47. calamitatum societates, ' association in the troubles (of others) '.

ll. 47-48. ad quas . . . descendant, ' which it is not easy to find (men) to come down to '.
Note : (i) **facile inventu,** *lit.* ' easy in the finding '. See Chap. III, l. 34, (ii) **qui descendant,** for the subjunctive, see **l. 34** above.

l. 48. Ennius. For Quintus Ennius (239–169 B.C.), see the note on Chap. VI, l. 23. He is often quoted by Cicero. For the alliteration as well as the sentiment, cf. our own proverb, ' A friend in need is a friend indeed '.

l. 50. haec duo, nominative case, ' these two actions ' ; they are explained in the following **si** clause.

ll. 53-55. **Qui . . . praestiterit, hunc . . . iudicare debemus.**
Note : (i) the relative clause precedes its antecedent **hunc.**
(ii) **praestiterit**, future-perfect.   Latin is more precise than
English in its use of tenses.   (iii) **ex maxime raro,** more
emphatic than the usual **ex rarissimo.**

CHAPTER XVIII

Line 1. **Firmamentum . . . fides.** eius belongs to **stabilitatis constantiaeque** (a hendiadys for ' firm constancy '), the
antecedent of **quam. fides** is the complement of **est.**

ll. 3-5. **Simplicem . . . eligi par est.**   Translate **eligi** (pres.
infin. pass.) as though it were active.   **qui . . . moveatur,** i.e.
' one who is stirred by the same motives '.   The subjunctive
is consecutive.

l. 8. **natura,** ablative, ' naturally '.

l. 9. **Addendum est eodem,** ' it should be added besides ',
lit. ' to the same thing '.

l. 11. **oblatis,** from **offerre** ;   the dative case is due to
credat, ' or believe (them when) brought ', i.e. by others.

l. 12. **iamdudum tracto,** ' I have been discussing for some
time '.   Laelius probably means from Chap. XVI, where he
begins the discussion on the limits to which friendship may
be carried.   Note the Latin idiom by which the *present* tense
is used of past actions that are continued into the present.
This is especially the case with **iam, iam diu,** etc.   Similarly
the imperfect is used in Latin where we have the pluperfect.

ll. 11-12. **ad eam . . . constantiam.**   The constancy of a
friend in this case consists both in not taking pleasure in
bringing charges against his friends and in not lending an
ear to charges brought by others.

l. 13. **initio,** i.e. in Section 18, Chap. V.

l. 15. **boni viri.**   For this genitive, cf. Chap. III. ll. 9-10.

l. 15. **quem . . . dicere,** ' whom we may also call the wise
man '.   Laelius is referring here to the opinion of the Stoic

school of philosophers, viz. that only the wise are good. See
also the note on Chap. V, l. 15.

l. 16. **haec duo,** ' these two rules '.

l. 17. **ne quid,** ' that nothing '. For the sentiment, see
Section 26, Chap. VIII, **in amicitia autem nihil fictum est,
nihil simulatum.**

l. 18. **ingenui.** For the genitive, see **boni viri** above.

l. 18. **fronte,** ' by a (false) expression '.

ll. 19-20. **ab aliquo adlatas criminationes,** ' charges (when)
brought forward by another ', direct object of **repellere.**

l. 20. **ne ipsum quidem,** ' not even oneself '.

l. 21. **semper aliquid existimantem . . . esse violatum,**
' (in) ever thinking that some wrong has been committed '.

l. 22. **Accedat huc suavitas quaedam oportet,** ' there
should be added to this (**huc**) a certain affability ', etc.

Note : (i) **accedere** is often used as the passive of **addo.**
(ii) **oportet** is here followed by the subjunctive—a common
use, which frequently replaces the more customary accusative and infinitive.

l. 25. **in omni re severitas,** ' seriousness on every occasion '
=' unvarying seriousness '.

CHAPTER XIX

Line 2. **num quando,** ' whether at any time '. This use
of **quando,** ' at any time ', after **si, num, ne,** corresponds to
the use of **quis, quid,** ' any one ', ' any thing ' after the same
conjunctions.

l. 4. **homine,** ' of a human being '. **indignus** like **dignus**
is followed in Latin by the ablative case.

l. 6. **Veterrima quaeque,** ' each oldest things ', i.e. ' every
old thing '. See the note on Chap. IV, ll. 14-15.

ll. 6-7. **ut ea vina quae . . . ferunt,** ' like those wines
which (can) bear age ' =' which can stand keeping '.

l. 10. **Novitates,** ' novelties ', i.e. ' new friendships '.

l. 11. **tamquam in herbis non fallacibus,** ' as in (the case of) shoots that-do-not-disappoint-us '.

l. 12. **illae quidem.** The demonstrative pronouns are frequently strengthened by **quidem.** Cf. Chap. XII, l. 10. Sometimes its use is restrictive, as here (=' it is true '), especially when there follows a contrasted second clause, which is introduced by **sed, sed tamen, tamen,** etc.

l. 12. **vetustas,** ' old-age ', i.e. ' old friendships '. Cf. **novitates** above.

l. 14. **in ipso equo,** ' in the case even of the horse '.

l. 15. **si nulla res impediat,** ' should nothing (else) prevent '.

l. 16. **nemo est quin . . . utatur,** ' there is no one who does not use ', i.e. ' everyone uses '. Note this use of **quin** =' who not ', which is found after negative clauses.

ll. 17-18. **in hoc quod est animal,** ' among living things '.

l. 19. **cum,** ' since '.

l. 20. **diutius.** Note the comparative, ' for some long time '.

l. 22. **parem esse inferiori,** ' that a man be equal to an inferior ', i.e. ' that a man should put himself on a level with those below him '.

l. 23. **excellentiae quaedam.** Note that in Latin abstract nouns are frequently used in the plural. This use often makes them concrete as in l. 10 above, where **novitates** =' new friendships '. In this case the plural seems to signify *points* of superiority rather than *one single* instance of that quality.

l. 24. **in nostro . . . grege,** ' in our set '. For **ut ita dicam,** introducing a word or phrase used in an unusual or metaphorical way, see the note on Chap. XV, l. 35. **grex** literally means ' a flock ', ' herd '.

l. 27. **Q. vero Maximum fratrem, i.e.** the brother of Scipio Aemilianus.

ll. 29-30. **suosque . . . volebat**, ' and wanted all his friends to be able through him to rise in importance '.

ll. 31-32. **quam praestantiam**, ' any superiority '.

l. 34. **parentibus humilibus**, ablative of origin.

l. 35. **vel animo vel fortuna**, ablative of respect, ' either in mind or fortune '.

l. 36. **eisque honori sint et dignitati**, ' and may be (for) an honour and distinction to them '. Note the datives **honori, dignitati**, dative of the object for which (predicative dative).

l. 37. **ut in fabulis**, ' as in legends '. A Roman reader would, of course, immediately think of the Romulus and Remus story.

l. 41. **duxerunt**, ' they considered '.

l. 41. **multo magis**, ' (by) much more '. Note **multo**, the ablative of the measure of difference.

l. 42. **in**, ' in the case of '.

l. 44. **maximus capitur**, ' is most fully enjoyed '.

l. 44. **in proximum quemque**. See Chap. XIX, l. 6, and Chap. IV, ll. 14-15.

CHAPTER XX

Line 3. **sic inferiores non dolere** ; supply **debent ;** ' so the inferior should not be distressed '.

l. 4. **ingenio, fortuna, dignitate** : ablatives of respect, ' in character ', etc.

ll. 5-6. **queruntur . . . exprobrant. aliquid** is an accusative of extent (degree). This accusative is confined to neuter adjectives and pronouns. Cf. **multa rogat,** ' he asks many questions '. So translate here : ' utter some complaint or reproach even '.

l. 6. **eoque magis**. For **eo**, see the note on Chap. I, l. 17.

ll. 7-8. **quod . . . dicere**, ' (something) which they can say has been done (=they have done) in a kind and friendly

way and with some effort on-their-part (suo) '. **queant,**
consecutive subjunctive, often found in relative clauses
with an indefinite antecedent.

l. 9. **officia exprobrantium,** ' who cast their services in
one's teeth '.

l. 13. **inferiores,** accusative case, object of **extollere.**

l. 15. **nisi,** ' except '.

l. 16. **contemnendos,** ' to be scorned ' = ' worthy of scorn '.

ll. 16-18. **qui hac opinione . . . levandi sunt,** ' who should
be relieved of this opinion '. Note **hac opinione,** ablative of
separation.

l. 17. **opere,** ' by action '.

ll. 18-19. **Tantum . . . quantum,** ' (only) as much (help)
. . . as '.

l. 20. **ille quem diligas atque adiuves,** ' the man whom you
love and so are helping '. The subjunctives **diligas** and
adiuves are consecutive.

l. 20. **sustinere.** Supply **possit.**

l. 21. **Non, neque tu,** ' No, not even you '.

l. 21. **possis,** potential subjunctive, ' could '.

l. 23. **fratrem . . . potuit.** Supply ' while ' or ' yet '
before this clause. For the asyndeton, see the notes on
Chap. XIV, ll. 7-9.

l. 24. **Quod si,** ' but if '.

l. 27. **Omnino,** ' as a rule '.

ll. 27-29. **amicitiae . . . sunt,** ' friendships are to-be-de-
cided-upon when character and age have been strengthened
and made firm '. For the plurals **ingeniis, aetatibus,** see the
note on Chap. XIX, l. 23.

ll. 29-30. **nec si qui . . . necessarios.** Translate **si qui** by
' those who ' and supply **debent** as the verb to **habere.**

ll. 30-31. **quos . . . dilexerunt,** ' whom they liked at that
time (tum) (because they were) possessed of the same pur-
suits '.

l. 32. paedagogi. These tutors were well educated slaves (usually of Greek origin), whose chief duty it was to take the boys of well-to-do families to and from school and generally look after them. From the nature of their association, the opportunities for influencing the character of their charges either for good or evil were immense ; and there is no doubt that very often deep and lasting friendships were formed between them. On the whole the **paedagogi** were probably treated more kindly than the average slave.

l. 32. iure vetustatis, ' by right of priority of acquaintance'.

l. 33. neglegendi quidem. This use of **quidem** (= ' it is true ') is rather like that explained in the note on Chap. XIX, l. 12.

l. 34. aliter, ' otherwise ' ; i.e. if friendships are not formed when judgment and age are mature. It refers back to l. 27.

ll. 37-38. nec ob aliam causam ullam, ' and (it is) for no other reason (that) '.

l. 39. nisi quod, ' except that '.

ll. 39-40. tanta . . . esse, ' there is between them such a great divergence . . . as there can be greatest ' = ' there is between them the greatest possible divergence '.

l. 43. intemperata quaedam benevolentia, ' a sort of uncontrolled goodwill '.

l. 44. magnas utilitates. For the plural of the abstract noun, see the note on Chap. XIX, l. 23.

l. 47. multis cum lacrimis, ' with many tears '. Remember that the ablative of manner is used with **cum** when there is no adjective ; with or without **cum** when it has an adjective.

l. 48. magnae res, ' important duties '.

l. 49. ut . . . amicis, ' that there is to be a separation from friends ' = ' resulting in a separation from one's friends '.

l. 49. quas, ' those duties '.

l. 50. quod . . . non ferat, ' because he cannot easily endure '. Note the subjunctive mood, sub-oblique.

l. 51. **natura,** ablative.

l. 52. **in amicitia parum iustus,** ' too-little fair in friendship ' =' is far from fair in friendship '. Laelius means that such a man expects the joys and benefits of friendship, yet he is not prepared to accept any sacrifice.

l. 54. **patiare** =patiaris, 2nd pers. sing. pres. subj.

CHAPTER XXI

Line 1. **quasi quaedam calamitas,** ' a sort of disaster '.

l. 2. **non nunquam necessaria,** ' (which is) sometimes inevitable '. In Chap. IX, l. 54, Laelius said that true friendships (which can exist only between the good) are eternal. Hence in discussing the causes which break up friendship, he has to point out in the next two lines that now they are dealing with ordinary friendships, not the intimacies of the wise.

l. 5. **tum . . . tum,** ' sometimes . . . sometimes '.

l. 6. **quorum . . . redundet.** The subjunctive is consecutive ; **quorum** =talia ut eorum, ' of such a kind that their (disgrace) '.

ll. 7-9. **eluendae . . . dissuendae . . . discindendae.** The metaphor in **eluendae** is that of *cleansing by washing* : it is changed in the next two words to dividing clothes by *unsewing the seams* (dissuere) and *rending them apart* (discindere).

ll. 10-12. **ut neque . . . facienda sit,** *lit.,* ' so that it is neither right nor honourable nor possible that an immediate (**statim**) estrangement and separation is not to-be-made '.

l. 15. **in rei publicae partibus dissensio,** ' a disagreement on politics ', *lit.,* ' on a party in the state '.

l. 17. **cavendum erit,** ' there will be care-to-be-taken ' =' care will have to be taken '. With intransitive verbs the *neuter* of the gerundive is used to express ' ought ', ' must ', ' should ', etc.

l. 17. ne, ' lest '.

ll. 18-19. non solum . . . videantur. Note that Latin uses **videri,** ' seem ', *personally*, whereas we prefer to use it *im*personally, i.e. in the 3rd person singular, ' it seems that '. See also Chap. V, l. 37.

l. 20. quicum, ' with whom '. For **qui** (ablative), see the notes on Chap. VI, l. 22 and l. 24.

l. 20. vixeris, probably perfect subjunctive, although it may be future-perfect.

l. 21. meo nomine, ' on my account '. Scipio broke off his friendship with Pompeius, because the latter had secured election to the consulship over the head of Laelius by giving out that he did not intend to stand as a candidate. In this way Laelius and his friends were thrown off their guard, and caught napping by Pompeius in the personal canvassing which was an important feature in all Roman elections.

l. 23. a collega nostro Metello. Laelius and Metellus were fellow-augurs. For the duties of the latter, see Chap. I, l. 1. The cause of the political quarrel between Scipio and Metellus is unknown.

l. 24. Utrumque egit, ' he did both things ' =' he acted on both occasions '. **Utrumque** is neuter.

l. 25. et offensione animi non acerba, ' and with no bitter indignation of feeling '. For this ablative of manner, see Chap. XX, l. 47.

l. 26. ne qua . . . discidia, ' lest any separation ' =' that no separation '.

ll. 27-28. ut exstinctae . . . videantur. Translate **videantur** *im*personally, ' it seems that '. See the note on l. 18 above.

ll. 30-31. ex quibus . . . gignuntur, ' from which . . . arise ', etc. =' which are the source of ', etc.

l. 32. hic honos, ' such respect '.

ll. 33-34. ut is in culpa . . . iniuriam, ' that he who does the offence, not he who suffers it, should be in the wrong '.

The meaning seems to be that an injured friend should not repay injury with injury and so put himself in the wrong ; on the contrary, it is better to suffer than to cause offence.

l. 35. **omnium ... incommodorum,** objective genitive, ' against all these ', etc.

l. 36. **una cautio atque una provisio,** ' (only) one precaution and (only) one safeguard '.

l. 37. **ut ne.** See Chap. XII, ll. 42-43.

l. 40. **nec quidquam,** ' nor anything ' = ' and nothing '.

l. 41. **quod sit ... perfectum,** ' (something) which is perfect '. The subjunctive is consecutive.

l. 44. **amicos ... eos ... diligunt.** Take **eos** with **amicos,** ' those friends above all **(potissimum)** '.

ll. 46-47. **pulcherrima illa et maxime naturali amicitia ...** **expetenda:** ablative case after **carent.**

l. 47. **per se et propter se expetenda,** ' to-be-desired (=desirable) in and for itself '.

ll. 48-49. **nec ... sit ;** order for translation, **nec sunt ipsi exemplo sibi qualis et quanta sit haec vis amicitiae. nec sunt ipsi exemplo sibi,** ' nor are they themselves (for) an example to themselves ', i.e. ' nor do they learn from their own experience '. **exemplo,** dative *of the object for which* (predicative).

l. 49. Laelius' illustration of the argument in the previous lines is drawn from self-love. Self-love, he points out, is a natural feeling, and has no ulterior motive of gain or profit. This example shows us the nature **(qualis)** and extent **(quanta)** of love.

ll. 51-52. **Quod idem,** neuter, ' this same feeling '.

l. 53. **est enim ... alter idem,** ' for he is such (is) as **(qui)** is a second self, so to speak ', i.e. ' for he is, so to speak, a second self '.

l. 56. **id,** ' that feeling '.

l. 58. **ad quas ... animantes ;** order for translation, **animantes eiusdem generis ad quas se applicent.** Note the subjunctive **applicent** (purpose), ' to attach themselves to '.

l. 60. **quanto magis,** ' (by) how much more '. Note **quanto,** ablative of the measure of difference.

l. 61. **natura,** ablative, ' naturally '.

l. 62. **cuius . . . misceat,** final subjunctive.

CHAPTER XXII

Line 1. **ne dicam,** ' not to say '.

l. 3. **quaeque . . . amicis ;** the relative clause, as often in Latin, precedes its antecedent, **haec.**

l. 5. **similem sui,** ' like oneself '. **similis** may be followed either by the genitive or ablative case.

l. 6. **In talibus ;** masculine ; ' in the (case of) such men '.

l. 6. **ea,** to be taken with **stabilitas.**

l. 6. **iamdudum tractamus.** For the tense (present for our perfect), see the note on Chap. XVIII, l. 12.

l. 10. **alter pro altero,** ' the one for the other ' =' for one another '. Similarly in l. 12, **alter ab altero** =' from one another '.

l. 13. **inter se,** ' among themselves ' =' each other ', which can be taken as the direct object of the three verbs **colent, diligent, verebuntur.** Latin possesses no reciprocal pronoun (' one another '), so uses **inter se,** or combinations of **alter alterum** as in the previous line.

l. 14. **tollit ;** the subject is the unexpressed antecedent of **qui . . . verecundiam,** ' the one '.

ll. 16-17. **libidinum . . . licentiam,** ' that in friendship there is open (=there is allowed) a freedom of (=for) all the lusts and sins '.

ll. 17-18. **virtutum adiutrix, non vitiorum comes,** ' (as) the helper of the virtues, not as the comrade of vice '.

l. 19. **quoniam . . . posset. quoniam,** ' since ', is followed by the indicative mood, unless the clause is subordinate in oratio obliqua, or, as here, the subjunctive mood is due to the influence of a nearby subjunctive **veniret** (purpose).

l. 19. **solitaria,** ' on her own '.

l. 20. **ad ea quae summa sunt,** ' to those things which are highest ' =' to her highest aims '.

l. 20. **pervenire,** dependent on posset, l. 19.

l. 20. **coniuncta et consociata,** ' (when) united and allied '.

l. 21. **Quae si quos inter societas,** ' if this (quae) union . . . among any '. **inter** governs **quos,** accusative plural of **quis** =' anyone ', after si, nisi, num, ne.

l. 23. **est habendus,** ' it should be considered '.

l. 23. **ad summum naturae bonum,** ' with regard to nature's highest good '.

l. 25. **insunt,** ' are found '.

l. 26. **expetenda,** ' to be sought ' =' worthy of search '.

l. 27. **ut,** ' so that '.

l. 29. **Quod,** ' this happiness ', or it might refer to **societas,** in which case it will mean ' this union '.

l. 32. **ea vero neglecta,** ablative absolute. Translate by conditional (' if ') clause.

l. 32. **qui,** ' (those) who '.

l. 34. **eos experiri,** ' to put them to the test '.

l. 35. **cum iudicaris (iudicaveris),** ' when you (will) have formed your judgment '.

ll. 37-38. **cum . . . tum,** ' both . . . and '.

l. 37. **plectimur,** ' we are punished '.

l. 39. **praeposteris . . . agimus,** *lit.* ' for we use plans in-reverse-order and do things (already) done '. Our proverbs which correspond to these sentiments are : ' to put the cart before the horse ', ' to flog a dead horse '.

l. 41. **ultro et citro,** *lit.* ' to and fro ' =' mutually '.

l. 42. **exorta aliqua offensione,** ' when some (cause of) offence has arisen '.

CHAPTER XXIII

Line 1, **Quo etiam magis,** ' even the more '. For **quo** (*lit.*
' by which '), ablative of the measure of difference, cf.
Chap. I, l. 17.

ll. 1-2. **rei . . incuria,** ' want of care in a matter most
indispensable '. **rei . . . necessariae,** objective genitive.

l. 4. **quamquam,** ' and yet '.

l. 7. **quos . . . delectat,** ' whom satisfied with little, a
meagre fare and style of living delights ', i.e. ' who . . . take
delight in a meagre . . . '.

l. 8. **honores vero,** ' as for political office '.

ll. 11-12. **permulti . . . putent,** ' there are very many who
value them at nothing ' = ' who consider them of no value '.
putent, consecutive subjunctive.

l. 15. **delectantur,** ' take delight in '.

l. 16. **otiosi,** ' free from public affairs ', i.e. not engaged
in public business.

l. 16. **totos,** ' entirely '.

l. 17. **sine . . . nullam,** ' namely that without friendship,
life is no life at all '. This statement is what all to a man
(ad unum) think.

l. 18. **liberaliter,** ' like a free man '.

l. 19. **nescio quomodo,** *lit.*, ' I know not how ', i.e. ' somehow or other '. See Chap. I, l. 46.

l. 22. **asperitate ea et immanitate,** ablative of description
or quality. **ea,** ' such '.

ll. 24-25. **qualem . . . accepimus :** order for translation,
qualem (as) **accepimus nescio quem Timonem fuisse Athenis.**

l. 25. **is pati non possit ut non anquirat,** ' he could not
endure that he seek not out ' = ' he could not refrain from
seeking out '.

l. 27. **hoc maxime iudicaretur,** ' this fact would best be
judged '.

l. 27. **quid tale,** ' something like this '.

l. 31. **abundantiam et copiam,** direct object of **suppeditans.** Translate as a hendiadys. Cf. Chap. XVIII., l. 1.

l. 32. **hominis adspiciendi,** ' of a fellow-being to be looked at ', i.e. ' of looking at a fellow-being '. Note that in the genitive case the gerundive construction is often used as an alternative to the gerund with a direct object, e.g. **hominem adspiciendi.** Cf. Chap. XVII, l. 19.

ll. 33-34. **ferreus ... ferre ... auferret.** Note the verbal punning—a rare practice in Latin authors.

l. 34. **cuique,** ' and from whom '.

l. 35. **illud,** ' that saying '.

ll. 35-37. **quod ... auditum ;** order for literal translation, **quod audivi nostros senes commemorare, auditum** (=which they had heard) **ab aliis senibus, solitum dici a Tarentino Archyta, ut opinor.**

l. 36. **a Tarentino ... solitum,** ' that it was accustomed to be said by . . . ' =' that it was a customary saying of '.

ll. 43-44. **in amicissimo quoque,** ' in a very close friend ', i.e. ' when found in a very close friend '.

CHAPTER XXIV

Line 1. **cum,** ' although ', as the following **tamen** shows.

l. 6. **dantur,** ' present themselves '.

ll. 6-7. **tum ... tum ... tum.** See Chap. XXI, l. 5.

l. 7. **sapientis est.** For the genitive, see Chap. XVI, l. 32.

l. 7. **offensio,** ' cause of offence '.

l. 10. **cum,** ' when '.

ll. 11-12. **in Andria ... dicit,** ' my friend says in his play " Andria " '. Laelius' friend was the comic poet Terence, a native of Carthage who reached Rome as a slave and was eventually freed. He belonged to the circle of Scipio and Laelius, and died at the early age of twenty-five.

ll. 16-17. **quod . . . sinit,** ' which in being indulgent to his sins, allows a friend to be borne headlong (to ruin) '.

l. 20. **Omni hac in re,** ' in this entire subject ' ; i.e. the subject of warning and reproving a friend (cf. l. 22).

l. 20. **habenda ratio et diligentia est,** ' reason and care is to be used '.

l. 22. **In obsequio autem,** ' in the case of complaisance, however ', i.e. as opposed to warning and reproving a friend.

l. 23. **lubenter utimur,** ' we (i.e. I) use gladly ' =' I am glad to use '.

l. 24. **adsit . . . amoveatur.** For the subjunctives (jussive), see Chap. XIII, l. 1.

ll. 26-27. **aliter . . . vivitur.** Note : (i) aliter . . . aliter, ' in one way . . . in another '. (ii) **vivitur,** a good example of an intransitive verb, used impersonally in the passive. Translate personally, ' *we* live '.

l. 26. **tyranno.** The tyrant is contrasted with the free man of l. 25. In friendship between free men, there is no place for flattery, for such obsequiousness is typical only of a tyrant's court.

ll. 27-29. **Cuius . . . est;** order for translation, **salus desperanda est huius cuius aures,** etc.

l. 29. **illud,** ' that (well-known saying) '.

l. 30. **ut multa,** ' as indeed (were) many (of his remarks) '.

ll. 30-31. **melius . . . eos amicos,** *lit.,* ' bitter enemies deserve better of some than those friends '. **melius mereri de,** ' deserve better of ' =' render better service to '; so translate accordingly.

ll. 34-35. **capiunt, eam capiunt,** a good example of asyndeton. For this and the necessity of inserting ' but ' or ' while ', see Chap. XIV, ll. 7-9. Similarly, insert ' but ' before **obiurgari** in the next line, and ' and ' before **correctione** in l. 37.

l. 36. **moleste ferunt,** ' they are annoyed '.

CHAPTER XXV

Lines 2-3. alterum . . . alterum, ' the one . . . the other ',
direct objects respectively of **facere** and **accipere,** and referring to **monere** and **moneri.**

l. 5. adulationem, blanditiam, assentationem, ' fawning,
cajolery, and flattery '. The slight difference in meaning
between these three words may be summarised thus :
adulatio, flattery by actions, e.g. ' bowing and scraping ' ;
blanditia, flattery in words (' soft-soaping '), and **assentatio,**
flattery by agreement (the ' yes-man ').

l. 6. quamvis multis nominibus, ' under as many names
as you like '.

l. 7. levium . . . , ' (as belonging to) fickle . . . '.

l. 8. ad voluptatem, ' with a view to pleasure '. Similarly
ad veritatem.

ll. 9, 11. Cum . . . tum, ' not only . . . but also '.

l. 9. omnium rerum, ' in any thing '.

l. 12. nomen amicitiae, ' the word friendship '. Latin
uses the genitive where English prefers apposition. For the
reverse idiom, cf. **urbs Roma** (apposition), ' the city of
Rome '.

l. 13. sit in eo ut, ' lies in this, that . . . '.

l. 14. qui, ' how ? ' For this form, see the note on Chap.
VI, l. 22.

l. 15. ne in uno quidem quoque, ' not even in each single
person '.

l. 18. ad, ' to suit '.

l. 21. Negat quis, etc. ' Someone says " no " ; so do I ;
he says " yes " ; so do I : in fine I bade myself agree with
him in everything '.

l. 23. in Gnathonis persona, ' in the character of Gnatho '.
The latter, a character in Terence's play, ' the Eunuchus ',
is a parasite or hanger-on. The lines above quoted by
Laelius might be described as his creed. The parasite was

a stock character in the plays of Terence's period. **Persona** literally means ' a mask '. As masks were worn by the actors, it came to be used of the characters on the stage.

l. 24. **amici genus,** ' that type of friend '.

l. 24. **levitatis.** For the genitive, see Chap. III, ll. 9-10.

l. 25. **Gnathonum similes,** ' like the Gnathos '. Note : (i) the genitive case after similis (cf. Chap. XXII, l. 5) ; (ii) the plural use of the proper noun.

l. 25. **cum,** causal, ' since '.

l. 27. **accessit.** See the note on Chap. XVIII, l. 22.

l. 29. **tam . . . quam,** ' just . . . as '.

l. 29. **adhibita diligentia,** ' care having been exercised ' =' with the exercise of care '.

l. 30. **fucata,** literally ' dyed ' =' false '.

l. 30. **Contio,** ' a public meeting ' ; in this case an assembly of the citizens in their tribes, which had been summoned by the magistrates to hear and vote upon proposals for new laws.

l. 32. **quid intersit,** ' what is the difference ' =' the difference '. Many indirect questions in Latin may be neatly turned by an abstract noun in English ; e.g. **nescio quot hostes sint,** ' I do not know how many the enemy are ' =' I do not know the enemy's numbers '.

l. 35. **C. Papirius,** i.e. Carbo. See the note on Chap. XII, l. 15.

l. 35. **in aures,** ' into the ears ' =' into the favour '.

l. 36. **cum . . . reficiendis,** ' when he tried to pass the law for the re-election of tribunes (*lit.* tribunes to-be-re-elected) '. Note : (i) **ferre legem,** ' to propose a law ', seems here to be used in the sense ' to pass a law '. (ii) The translation of the imperfect tense **ferret.** For this incident, see the note on Chap. XII, l. 15 and l. 20. Although Carbo was unsuccessful on this occasion, 131 B.C., he succeeded a few years later, i.e. some time after the supposed date of this dialogue (129 B.C.).

l. 36. **Dissuasimus**, an example of the so-called editorial ' we ' : translate by 1st person singular.

l. 38. **illi**, dative singular (dative of the possessor).

ll. 39-40. **ut facile . . . diceres**, ' how readily you would have said ! '.

l. 40. **non comitem**, ' not the comrade '. At this time Scipio held no magistracy : he was ' **privatus** ' and therefore had no more power than any other ordinary citizen.

l. 41. **lex popularis**, ' this " people's " law '. ¹

l. 43. **meministis**, parenthetical.

ll. 43-44. **Q. Maximo . . . consulibus**, ' in the consulship of Quintus Maximus . . . ' ; i.e. in 145 B.C.

l. 46. **Cooptatio collegiorum**, ' the right to co-opt in the colleges (or guilds) '. It will be seen from this phrase that vacancies in the priestly colleges (i.e. of Pontifices and Augures) were normally filled by the choice of the existing members, **co-optatio** (English co-option). Licinius Crassus proposed, however, that the right to elect members to these colleges should be transferred to the people, i.e. to the issue of a popular vote, a method of election which was, of course, more democratic. Membership of these colleges gave indirectly political prestige and power. Thus Laelius, as a representative of the governing classes, opposed Licinius' bill and succeeded in getting it rejected.

ll. 47-48. **atque . . . populo**, ' and moreover he was the first to begin the practice of turning towards the forum while addressing the people ', *lit.*, ' he first began, turned towards the forum, to address the people '. The emphasis falls on the perfect participle **versus** : hence the translation given above. Apparently public meetings were held in a small area on the north side of the forum, bounded on one side by the Curia or Senate House. Normally then a speaker would be inclined to face the Senate House when addressing a meeting. Licinius Crassus, however, is credited here with the practice when speaking of turning to the

¹ Translation by W. A. Falconer.

Forum, where a larger crowd was probably assembled. Thus his back would be towards the Senate House, and his whole attitude in turning away from the Curia and facing the Forum could be interpreted as a challenge to senatorial authority. According to Plutarch, C. Gracchus was the first to do this.

l. 49. **religio deorum,** ' reverence for the gods '. **deorum,** a good example of an objective genitive.

l. 50. **nobis defendentibus.** For the use of the plural, see the note on l. 36 above.

ll. 52-53. **re magis quam summa auctoritate,** ' by its own merits rather than by the highest influence (=by the influence of the highest office) ', i.e. of the consulship. Laelius has just said that he was praetor at this time and did not become consul until five years later. Thus he infers that it must have been the merits of the case, not his own influence that won the day.

CHAPTER XXVI

Lines 1-2. **in qua . . . est,** ' in which there is the most (of) room for invention and half-truths '. **res adumbratae,** *lit.*, ' things sketched in outline '.

l. 4. **quae . . . perpenditur,** ' which is entirely weighed by whole truth (i.e. is valued altogether according to its truth) '.

l. 7. **ne amare quidem aut amari,** ' not even loving or being-loved ', direct object of the preceding **habeas.** Note that in Latin the infinitive supplies the nominative and accusative (when object of verbs) of the verbal noun or gerund.

l. 8. **cum . . . ignores,** ' since you do not know what it truly is '.

l. 10. **ea,** ablative feminine singular, ' by it ', i.e. flattery **(assentatio).**

ll. **12-13. qui . . . delectet,** ' who is most given to self-flattery and is most satisfied with himself ' (Tr. by W. A. Falconer).

l. **19. ad ipsorum voluntatem,** ' to suit their wish ', i.e. of being thought virtuous.

l. **25. milites gloriosi,** ' braggart soldiers '. Together with the parasites, they were stock characters of the writers of comedies, who got many a laugh by playing off the parasite's servility and flattery against the bluff soldier's loud-voiced boastfulness. Laelius has in mind Thraso (=Captain Bluster) from Terence's play the *Eunuchus,* from which he quotes the line in the text : ' in truth did Thais send me many thanks '. Thais is the name of the much-courted woman in the play.

l. **27. ingentes, inquit,** ' " thousands of them ", says the parasite '.

l. **30. blanda ista vanitas,** *lit.,* ' that flattering emptiness ' =' that empty flattery '.

l. **34. nemo non videt,** ' no one does not-see ' =' no one fails to see '.

l. **35. callidus ille et occultus ;** supply **assentator.**

l. **36. studiose cavendum est ;** supply **nobis.** ' We must diligently take care.'

l. **37. quippe qui,** ' inasmuch as he '. Note that the causal use of the relative pronoun can be strengthenend by **quippe.** The mood is always subjunctive (**assentetur**).

l. **38. litigare se simulans,** ' (by) pretending to quarrel '. Note that this use of the present participle is almost equivalent to that of the ablative of the gerund **adversando** in l. 37.

l. **39. det manus,** ' gives in '. The metaphor is taken from the offering of one's hand as a sign of surrender.

l. **40. plus vidisse,** ' to have seen more ' =' to have seen more deeply into the matter '. The argument is concerned with the cunning flatterer whose tactics are not so obvious as the man who flatters openly. First he disagrees and pretends to quarrel, only finally to give up the struggle in favour of his friend whose arguments, he says, have been too good for him.

l. 42. **ut in Epiclero,** ' as in the Epiclerus '. The latter is the title of a Greek play by Menander (c. 350 B.C.) and means ' the Heiress '. It was translated into Latin by Caecilius Statius.

l. 43. **comicos stultos senes,** ' foolish old men of the comedy stage ' = ' old fools of the comedy stage '. See l. 42 above. In the Greek comedies of the fourth century and later, which were translated or adapted for production on the Roman stage by Plautus and Terence, ' old fools ' were often the dupes of their spendthrift sons and crafty slaves.

l. 44. **Versaris** (=**versaveris**) **et emunxeris.** Perfect subjunctives in a consecutive clause introduced by ut. **emunxeris,** *lit.*, ' you have wiped my nose ', a slang expression for ' you have befooled me '.

l. 46. **improvidorum,** ' (namely that) of . . . '.

l. 50. **ad illa prima,** ' to those first (principles I mentioned) ', viz. that friendship is possible only among the good. See Section 18.

CHAPTER XXVII

Line 2. **In ea ;** supply **virtute.**

l. 3. **convenientia rerum,** ' harmony of things ' = ' harmony in everything ' = ' complete harmony '.

l. 8. **est ab amando,** ' are derived from the verb " to love " '. Cf. Section 26, **amor enim, ex quo amicitia nominata est.**

ll. 9-10. **nulla . . . quaesita,** *lit.*, ' no need, no advantage having been sought ' = ' without seeking any need or advantage '. This question is discussed fully in Chap. VIII.

l. 11. **minus,** for this use of minus (almost = ' not '), see Chap. VII, l. 14 ; Chap. XVI, l. 56 ; Chap. XVII, l. 5.

l. 12. **Hac benevolentia,** ' it was with this sort of affection ', or, as an ablative of cause, ' it was by reason of ', etc.

l. 14. **Ti. Gracchum, Scipionis nostri socerum.** As he was the father-in-law of Scipio, this Tiberius Gracchus must be the father of the Tiberius mentioned in Sections 36, 37. The latter was the brother-in-law of Scipio.

l. 15. **Haec,** supply **benevolentia.**

l. 18. **acquiescimus,** ' we find pleasure in ' ; *lit.*, ' we rest'.

l. 18. **ut in vestra,** ' as in that of you two '. The adjective is plural because Laelius is referring to both Scaevola and Fannius.

ll. 23-25. **ut . . . pervenire,** order for translation, **ut possis, ut dicitur, pervenire ad calcem cum aequalibus, cum isdem quibuscum emissus sis e carceribus.**

l. 24. **e carceribus . . . ad calcem.** The metaphor of the ' race of life '—a common one—is taken here from the chariot races which were a popular feature of the Roman Games in the Roman Circus. The **carceres** were the starting stalls from which the chariots proceeded to the **calx** (or white line), which was both the starting line and finishing post, for the racecourse was oval in shape, divided by what was called the **spina.** From the **carceres** back to the **calx** was then the complete course.

l. 32. **quae,** ' and that ', i.e. his virtue.

ll. 35-37. **Nemo . . . suscipiet qui . . . non putet,** ' no one will undertake . . . who does not think . . . ', i.e. ' without thinking '.

l. 40. **In hac,** supply **amicitia.**

ll. 41-42. **rerum privatarum consilium,** ' counsel in private affairs '.

l. 44. **quod quidem senserim,** ' so far as I was aware ', or ' to the best of my knowledge '. Note the subjunctive mood, which is found in restrictive phrases of this type.

l. 50. **ab oculis,** ' from the gaze '.

l. 54. **illa,** neuter plural, and referring to **recordatio et memoria.**

l. 56. **adfert.** After the protasis **si . . . orbatus essem** one would expect the pluperfect or imperfect subjunctive **attulisset** or **adferret.** The use of the indicative, however, expresses as a *fact* what would otherwise be a *conditional statement* ; in this way Laelius emphasises the comfort and consolation he *does* receive.

l. 57. **diutius,** ' (much) longer '.

l. 57. **in hoc desiderio,** ' in this state of yearning '.

ll. 60-61. **ita . . . locetis,** ' rank so highly '.

l. 62. **ea excepta,** ablative absolute, ' virtue excepted '.

l. 62. **amicitia,** ablative of comparison.

VOCABULARY

(In the following vocabulary only irregular verbs are given their principal parts in full. Otherwise the figures (1), (2), (3), (4) following a verb denote that it is a regular example of that conjugation. No conjugation number is given in the case of -io verbs like capio.*)*
The numbers attached to meanings refer to Sections.

a *or* **ab**, *prep. with abl.*, by ; from.
abduco (3), lead away ; *in pass.*, hold aloof from (8).
abhorreo (2), shrink from.
abicio, -ere, -ieci, -iectum, throw away ; abase (32) ; **abiectus**, cast down, depressed.
absens, -ntis, absent.
absum, -esse, afui, be absent ; **tantum abest**, it is so far from being the case.
absurdus, -a, -um, absurd, unreasonable.
abundantia, -ae, *f.*, abundance, full supply.
abundo (1), abound, be rich.
ac, and, and moreover.
accedo, -cessi, -cessum (3), go towards, approach ; be added (12, 66, 94).
accepta et data, *neut. pl.*, credits and debits.
accessio, -ionis, *f.*, an addition.
accido, -cidi (3), happen.
accipio, -ere, -cepi, -ceptum, receive ; hear, learn (*of news*) ; accept (40).

accuratus, -a, -um, carefully prepared, studied.
acer, -cris, -cre, sharp, keen, rapid.
acerbe, *adv.*, bitterly.
acerbitas, -atis, *f.*, bitterness.
acerbus, -a, -um, bitter.
acquiesco, -evi, -etum (3), find pleasure in.
acriter, *adv.*, sternly, with severity.
actio, -ionis, *f.*, course of action.
acute, *adv.*, acutely, keenly, shrewdly.
ad, *prep. with acc.*, to, up to, towards ; **ad extremum** (99), at last ; **ad vesperum** (12), at evening ; **ad normam** (18), according to the standard.
addo, -didi, -ditum (3), add.
adduco (3), lead to, bring to ; induce (59) ; draw in, tighten (*of reins*) (45).
adeo, -ire, -ii, -itum, go to, approach.
adfero, -ferre, attuli, adlatum, bring, bring forward (37, 65) ; use (26).

adficio, -ere, -feci, -fectum, dispose.

adfluens, -ntis, lavish.

adhibeo (2), apply (29) ; use, employ (**60, 62, 95**) ; admit (93).

adhuc, *adv.*, as yet, hitherto.

adipiscor, -eptus (3), obtain, get, acquire.

adiumentum, -i, *n.*, assistance, aid.

adiungo, -nxi, -nctum (3), join to, add to.

adiutor, -oris, *m.*, helper ; supporter ; *fem.* **adiutrix, -tricis.**

adiuvo, -iuvi, -iutum (1), help, assist.

adlecto (1), court, fish for.

adlicio, -ere, -lexi, -lectum, entice, attract.

adligo (1), bind.

adminiculum, -i, *n.*, support, prop.

admirabilis, -e, wonderful, amazing ; worthy of admiration (86).

admiratio, -ionis, *f.*, wonder, admiration (88) ; astonishment (2).

admodum, *adv.*, much, very, considerably.

admoneo (2), warn, admonish.

admoveo, -movi, -motum (2), move to *or* towards.

adnitor, -nixus *or* **nisus** (3), lean upon.

adscisco, -ivi, -itum (3), attach to.

adspicio, -ere, -spexi, -spectum, look at, behold.

adsum, -esse, -fui, be present.

adulatio, -ionis, *f.*, adulation.

adulescens, -entis, *m.*, young man.

adulescentia, -ae, *f.*, adolescence, manhood.

adulor (1), flatter.

adultero (1), vitiate, falsify.

adumbro (1), *lit.*, sketch in outline.

adversor (1), oppose.

adversus, -a, -um, opposite, adverse ; **res adversae,** *pl.*, adversity.

adverto, -ti, -sum (3), turn ; with **animum,** perceive, notice.

aedificium, -i, *n.*, building.

aequalis, -e, equal ; of his (their) own age (37) ; *as a noun,* men of the same age (101).

aequaliter, *adv.*, equally, on equal terms.

aeque, *adv.*, equally, as much . . . as (22).

aequitas, -atis, *f.*, fairness, reasonableness.

aequus, -a, -um, fair, right.

aestimo (1), reckon, value (74).

aetas, -atis, *f.*, age, time (87), time of life.

ager, -gri, *m.*, field.

agnosco, -novi, -nitum (3), recognise, admit.

ago, egi, actum (3), do (96), act (77) ; proceed (19), **agere cum,** urge upon ; plead ; **agere cum populo** (96), address the people.

agrestis, -e, of the land.

Agrigentinus, -a, -um, of Agrigentum (a town in Sicily).

aio, ais, ait, aiunt, say ; say ' yes ' (93).

alias, *adv.*, at another time; alias ... alias, sometimes ... at others.

alienatio, -ionis, *f.*, estrangement.

alieno (1), estrange.

alienus, -a, -um, belonging to another, foreign; alienus ab (28), hostile to; *as a noun*, stranger.

aliquamdiu, *adv.*, for some time.

aliquando, *adv.*, at some time; sooner or later (100).

aliquantulum, *adv.*, somewhat.

aliqui, -qua, -quod, *adj.*, some, any; a sort of.

aliquis, -qua, quid, *pronoun*, some-one, something; any-one, anything; *as adj.*, in 83, some.

aliter, *adv.*, otherwise, in a different manner; aliter ... aliter (89), in one way ... in another.

alius, -a, -ud, other; nihil aliud (20), nothing else; alii ... alii, some ... others.

alo, alui, altum (3), nourish, support.

alter, -era, -erum, another (*of two*), second; alter ... alter, the one ... the other.

altus, -a, -um, high, lofty.

amabilis, -e, loveable, amiable.

amans, -ntis, loving, fond.

amantissime, *superl. adv.*, on the most loving terms.

ambitiosus, -a, -um, ambitious, selfish.

amentia, -ae, *f.*, madness, folly.

amice, *adv.*, in a friendly manner.

amicitia, -ae, *f.*, friendship.

amicus, -i, *m.*, friend; *also as adj.*, friendly.

amitto, -misi, -missum (3), lose.

amo (1), love, like.

amor, -oris, *m.*, love.

amoveo, -movi, -motum (2), move away, remove.

amplifico (1), increase, enlarge.

amplus, -a, -um, great, important.

an, *interrog. particle*, or?; *in the phrase* haud scio an = whether.

ango, anxi, (3), pain, grieve, torment.

angor, -oris, *m.*, pain.

angustus, -a, -um, narrow.

animadverto, -ti, -sum (3), perceive, notice; be on one's guard (99).

animal, -alis, *n.*, living thing.

animans, -ntis, *m.*, *or f.*, living being.

animatus, -a, -um, disposed.

animus, -i, *m.*, mind, feeling (26), spirit (23), courage (102); soul (13, 14, 92).

annus, -i, *m.*, year.

anquiro, -quisivi, -quisitum (3), seek out.

ansa, -ae, *f.*, handle.

ante, *prep. with acc.*, before; *adv.*, before, first, earlier.

antea, *adv.*, formerly, previously.

ante-eo, -ire, -ii, -itum, go before, precede; aetate anteire (69), to be older.

antepono, -posui, -positum (3), place before, prefer.

antequam, before, before that.

anteverto, -ti, -sum (3), anticipate, forestall.

antiquus, -a, -um, ancient, old; *as noun,* **antiqui, -orum,** the ancients.

aperte, *adv.,* openly, candidly.

apertus, -a, -um, open.

appareo (2), be clear, be manifest.

appello (1), call, name.

appetens, **-ntis,** eager for (+gen.).

appeto, -petivi, -petitum (3), seek for, long for, desire, aim at (36).

applicatio, -ionis, *f.,* inclination.

applico (1), fasten to, attach.

aptus, -a, -um, fitting, suitable, suited.

apud, *prep. with acc.,* with, among ; at the house of.

aqua, -ae, *f.,* water.

arbitratus, -us, *m.,* will, way.

arbitrium, -i, *n.,* will, authority.

arbitror (1), think, consider.

arguo, -ui, -utum (3), accuse, convict.

argutiae, -arum, *f. pl.,* subtleties.

arma, -orum, *n. pl.,* arms.

ascendo, -ndi, -nsum (3), ascend.

Asia, -ae, *f.,* Asia.

aspere, *adv.,* harshly.

asperitas, -tatis, *f.,* roughness, severity, austerity.

aspernor (1), reject, scorn.

assentatio, -ionis, *f.,* servility, flattery.

assentator, -oris, *m.,* flatterer, time-server.

assentior, -sensus (4), agree with.

assentor (1), agree with (+dat.) (13, 93) ; flatter (61) *(with dat.,* 97).

assequor, -secutus (3), attain.

assolet (2), it is customary, usual.

Athenae, -arum, *f. pl.,* Athens.

atque, and, and moreover ; *(after comparatives)* than.

attineo, -ui, -tentum (2), *impers.,* concern, be of consequence to ; **quid attinet (39),** what need to?

attraho, -traxi, -tractum, draw to, attract.

auctoritas, -tatis, *f.,* influence, authority, weight of position.

audacia, -ae, *f.,* audacity, insolence.

audeo, ausus sum (2), dare, venture.

audio (4), hear, listen to.

aufero, -ferre, abstuli, ablatum, take away.

augeo, auxi, auctum (2), increase.

augur, -uris, *m.,* augur.

auguror (1), prophesy.

auris, -is, *f.,* ear.

aut, or ; **aut ... aut,** either ... or.

autem, but, however, moreover.

averto, -ti, -sum (3), turn away.

beate, *adv.,* happily.

beatus, -a, -um, happy, fortunate, prosperous.

bellum, -i, *n.,* war.

belua, -ae, *f.,* beast.

bene, *adv.,* well, virtuously.

beneficium, -i, *n.,* kindness; patronage (96).

beneficus, -a, -um, generous, kind.

benevole, *adv.,* kindly, in a friendly spirit.

benevolentia, -ae, *f.,* goodwill, kindness, affection.

bestia, -ae, *f.,* animal, beast.

biennium, -i, *n.* (*a space of*) two years.

bis, *adv.,* twice.

blandior (4), fawn on, flatter.

blanditia, -ae, *f.,* cajolery, fawning.

blandus, -a, -um, flattering, winning, enticing.

bonitas, -tatis, *f.,* goodness, kindness (47).

bonum, -i, *n.,* the good.

bonus, -a, -um, good ; **bonae res** (64), prosperity.

brevis, -e, short ; *adv.,* **breviter,** shortly, briefly.

cado, cecidi, casum (3), fall ; fail (23) ; **cadere in,** befall.

caducus, -a, -um, perishable, fleeting.

caecus, -a, -um, blind.

caelum, -i, *n.,* heaven.

calamitas, -tatis, *f.,* calamity, disaster, ruin.

calamitosus, -a, -um, unfortunate, ruined.

calculus, -i, *m.* (a pebble) ; reckoning.

callidus, -a, -um, cunning, crafty.

calx, calcis, *f.,* (chalk) ; goal.

capio, -ere, cepi, captum, take ; gain, obtain (25, 32) ; reap (70) ; feel (48, 90) ; take in, deceive (99).

capitalis, -e, mortal, deadly.

Capitolium, -i, *n.,* the Capitol.

capra, -ae, *f.,* she-goat.

caput, -itis, *n.,* head, life, civil status (61) ; chief point, essential (45).

carcer, -eris, *m.* (prison) ; in *pl.,* starting stalls (*in chariot-racing*).

careo (2) (+abl.), be without, lack ; be free from (10, 22, 89) ; lose, miss (80).

caritas, -tatis, *f.,* affection (20, 27) ; feeling (32).

carmen, -inis, *n.* (song), poem.

carus, -a, -um, dear.

casus, -us, *m.,* chance (42), fortune (7) ; trouble, misfortune (40, 84) ; **ullo casu** (8), by any chance.

causa, -ae, *f.,* cause, reason ; abl., **causā** (*as prep. following its case, gen.*), for the sake of.

cautio, -ionis, *f.,* precaution.

cavea, -ae, *f.,* theatre.

caveo, cavi, cautum (2), take care, beware of.

celeber, -bris, -bre, distinguished, festive.

celeritas, -tatis, *f.,* suddenness.

censeo, censui, censum (2), think (14), advise, suggest (17).

censura, -ae, *f.,* censorship.

cerno, crevi, cretum (3), perceive.

certamen, -inis, *n.,* rivalry, contest.

certatio, -ionis, *f.,* rivalry.

certe, *adv.,* at least, certainly, at any rate.

certus, -a, -um, certain, sure.

ceterus, -a, -um, the other, remaining, the rest.

cicur, -uris, tame.

circumfluo, -fluxi (3), (flow around) ; be rich in (52).

cito, *adv.*, quickly.

citro, *adv.*, in this direction ; ultro et citro (85), in every direction.

civilis, -e, of a citizen, civil.

civis, -is, *m.*, citizen.

civitas, -tatis, *f.*, state, nation.

clamor, -oris, *m.*, cry, shout.

clarus, -a, -um, famous, illustrious ; brilliant.

claudo, -si, -sum (3), shut.

coepi, -isse, coeptus sum, began.

cogitatio, -ionis, *f.*, thought, meditation, reflection.

cogito, (1), think, reflect ; devise (60).

cognitio, -ionis, *f.*, knowing ; omnium cognitio, general enquiry or study ; knowledge, science (86).

cognomen, -inis, *n.*, surname.

cognosco, -gnovi, -gnitum (3), learn, discover, ascertain ; recognise (63, 70).

cogo, coegi, coactum (3), force, compel.

collega, -ae, *m.*, colleague.

collegium, -i, *n.*, college, guild.

colligo, -legi, -lectum (3), (collect), gain, acquire.

colloco (1), place, station.

colo, colui, cultum (3), cultivate (51) ; court (53) ; cherish (30, 82) ; honour (22, 69).

comes, -itis, *m.* and *f.*, companion, comrade.

comicus, -a, -um, comic, of the comic stage.

comitas, -tatis, *f.*, courtesy.

comitatus, -us, *m.*, comradeship, companionship.

commemini, -isse, recollect entirely.

commemoro (1), mention.

commentor (1), practise (*augural art*).

commode, *adv.*, suitably, to the point.

commoditas, -tatis, *f.*, advantage.

commodus, -a, -um, convenient, advantageous ; affable (54) ; *as a noun*, commodum, -i, *n.*, advantage (34) ; interest (57).

commoror (1), stay, dwell.

commoveo, -movi, -motum (2), move deeply.

communico (1), share.

communis, -e, common (15) ; ordinary (77) ; had in common (103) ; affable (65) ; vita communis (18, 38), everyday life.

communitas, -tatis, *f.*, community, fellowship.

commutabilis, -e, changeable.

commutatio, -ionis, *f.*, change.

commuto (1), change completely.

comoedia, -ae, *f.*, comedy.

comparo (1), form (60) ; arrange (101) ; compare (103).

complector, -plexus (3), embrace.

concedo, -cessi, -cessum (3), yield, grant, allow ; concessus, *perf. part. pass.*, permissible.

conciliatrix, -icis, *f.*, (that which unites), promoter.

concilio (1), form, fashion.

concludo, -clusi, -clusum (3), bring to a conclusion.

concordia, -ae, *f.*, union, harmony (*of feeling*).

condicio, -ionis, *f.*, (compact); (marriage) engagement.

condimentum, -i, *n.*, flavouring, spice, sauce.

confero, -ferre, -tuli, collatum, bestow, confer; **se conferre,** betake oneself to; **se conferre ad,** devote oneself to.

confido, -fisus sum (3), +*dat.*, feel confidence (in); trust in.

confirmo (1), strengthen; establish firmly, state confidently **(10).**

congero, -gessi, -gestum (3), heap upon.

conglutino (1), (glue together); unite securely.

congressus, -us, *m.*, society.

congruo, -ui (3), be in harmony with.

co(n)icio, -ere, -ieci, -iectum, (throw together); **oculos conicere (8),** turn, fix one's gaze.

coniunctio, -ionis, *f.*, union, bond **(23),** intimacy **(71).**

coniuncte, *adv.*, *superl.* coniunctissime, most intimately, on the most intimate terms.

coniunctus, -a, -um, united, intimate, friendly.

coniungo, -nxi, -nctum (3), join together, unite; establish **(26).**

conor (1), try, attempt.

conquiesco, -quievi, -quietum (3), repose, rest.

conscisco, -scivi, -scitum (3), mortem sibi consciscere, commit suicide (*lit.*, decree death for oneself).

conscribo, -scripsi, -scriptum (3), enrol.

conscripti, -orum, *m. pl.*, patres conscripti, the Senate.

consensio, -ionis, *f.*, agreement.

consensus, -us, *m.*, agreement.

consentaneus, -a, -um, reasonable.

consentio, -sensi, -sensum (4), agree (with).

consequor, -secutus (3), follow (*intrans.*) **(30)**; obtain, attain.

conservo (1), preserve.

considero (1), consider, reflect upon.

consilium, -i, plan, design, purpose **(61)**; advice **(44, etc.)**; enquiry **(37).**

consocio (1), associate.

consolor (1), console, comfort.

constans, -ntis, constant, firm.

constanter, *adv.*, with constancy, firmly.

constantia, -ae, *f.*, constancy, stability **(19),** steadfastness **(100).**

constituo, -stitui, -stitutum (3), regulate, settle; determine **(56).**

consto, -stiti, -statum (1), be fixed **(24)**; **constat ex (25),** is composed of; *imperson.*, it is agreed **(50).**

consuesco, -suevi, -suetum (3),

grow accustomed ; *in perfect tense,* be accustomed.

consuetudo, -inis, *f.,* custom, habit ; intimacy, familiarity (**29, 30**) ; political custom (**40**).

consul, -ulis, *m.,* consul.

consulatus, -us, *m.,* consulship.

consulo, -ului, -ultum (3), + *dat.,* have regard to, consult interests of.

contemno, -tempsi, -temptum (3), despise, scorn ; *perf. part. pass.,* contemptus, despicable, vile.

contendo, -di, -tum (3), demand, ask, seek.

contentio, -ionis, *f.,* rivalry.

contentus, -a, -um, content, satisfied.

contero, -trivi, -tritum (3), spend (*of time*).

contineo, -tinui, -tentum (2), contain, uphold (**20**), embrace (**22**).

contingo, -tigi, -tactum, happen.

continuo, *adv.,* at once, forthwith.

contio, -ionis, *f.,* public meeting, popular assembly.

contra, *prep. with acc.,* opposite, against, contrary to ; *as adv.,* on the other hand, on the contrary.

contraho, -traxi, -tractum (3), (draw together), unite (**24**) ; cement (**48**) ; contract (**20, 48**).

contrarius, -a, -um, contrary, opposite.

contumacia, -ae, *f.,* obstinacy.

contumelia, -ae, *f.,* invective ; insulting language.

convenientia, -ae, *f.,* harmony, agreement.

conveniens, -ntis, adapted to.

converto, -ti, -sum (3), change.

convinco, -vici, -victum (3), convict.

cooptatio, -ionis, *f.,* co-option.

copia, -ae, *f.,* supply, plenty ; *in pl.,* riches.

cor, cordis, *n.,* heart

coram, *prep. with abl.,* in the presence of ; *adv.,* openly, face to face.

corpus, -oris, *n.,* body ; flesh (**14**).

correctio, -ionis, *f.,* correction.

corroboro (1), strengthen.

credo, -didi, -ditum (3), believe, think ; *also with dat.,* believe.

credulus, -a, -um, credulous.

crimen, -inis, *n.,* charge, accusation.

criminatio, -ionis, *f.,* charge, accusation.

crudelitas, -tatis, *f.,* cruelty, barbarity.

culpa, -ae, *f.,* fault.

cultus, -us, *m.,* cultivation (**23**) ; dress (**49**) ; style of living (**86**).

cum, *prep. with abl.,* with.

cum, *conjunction,* when, since, although ; cum ... tum, not only ... but also ; both ... and.

Cumanus, -a, -um, of Cumae (*Greek colony on the coast of Campania*).

cunctatio, -ionis, *f.,* hesitation, delay.

cupiditas, -tatis, *f.,* passion, desire.

cupio, -ere, cupivi, cupitum, desire.

cur, why?

cura, -ae, *f.,* care, anxiety, solicitude.

curriculum, -i, *n.,* course.

cursus, -us, *m.,* journey **(14)** ; course **(63, 85).**

custodia, -ae, *f.,* imprisonment.

de, *prep. with abl.,* from, concerning, about.

debeo (2), owe, ought, must.

debilito (1), weaken.

decerto (1), fight, struggle.

decessus, -us, *m.,* death, decease.

declaro (1), declare, make plain.

declino (1), swerve, deviate.

deduco (3), introduce.

defendo, -fendi, -fensum (3), defend, speak in defence of.

defero, -ferre, -tuli, -latum, confer upon.

deficio, -ere, -feci, -fectum, revolt *or* fall from.

definio (4), limit.

deflecto, -flexi, -flexum (3), swerve.

defluo, -fluxi, -fluxum (3), flow down, overflow **(58)** ; drift **(100).**

dego, degi (3), spend *(of time).*

deinde, *adv.,* then, secondly, next.

delabor, -lapsus (3) (slip down), descend.

delecto (1), delight, please ; *in pass.,* take pleasure in.

deleo, -evi, -etum (2), destroy, wipe out; put an end to **(11).**

deliciae, -arum, *f. pl.,* pleasures, delights, luxury.

delictum, -i, *n.,* sin, fault.

deligo, -legi, -lectum (3), choose, select.

denique, *adv.,* lastly, at last, in fine.

depono, -posui, positum (3), lay aside, give up.

deprecor (1), beg off ; sue for pardon.

derelinquo, -liqui, -lictum (3), abandon entirely.

descendo, -ndi, -nsum (3), descend, come down **(64).**

desero, -serui, -sertum (3), desert, abandon, disregard.

desertus, -a, -um, lonely, deserted.

desiderium, -i, *n.,* yearning, longing for.

desidero (1), long for **(26)** ; feel the need of **(29)** ; desire **(82).**

despero (1), despair of, give up for lost.

despicio, -ere, -spexi, -spectum, look down upon, despise.

desum, -esse, -fui, +*dat.,* be wanting to, fail.

deterrimus, -a, -um, worst.

detestabilis, -e, abominable, execrable.

detraho, -traxi, -tractum (3), lose, forego.

deus, -i, *m.,* a god.

devius, -a, -um, uncertain, erratic.

dico, -xi, -ctum, (3), say, speak, mention.

dictum, -i, *n.,* saying, word.

dies, -ei, *m.,* or *f.,* day ; in dies (41), daily.

difficilis, -e, difficult, troublesome, hard.

difficile, *adv., superl.* **difficillime,** with the greatest difficulty (64).

diffluo (3), (flow away) ; be abandoned to (52).

diffundo, -fudi, -fusum (3), expand.

dignitas, -tatis, *f.,* rank, importance, position (12, 71) ; distinction (70).

dignus, -a, -um, worthy ; + *abl.,* worthy of.

diligens, -ntis, diligent, painstaking.

diligentia, -ae (*f.*), care.

diligenter, *adv., superl.* **diligentissime,** diligently, carefully.

diligo, -lexi, -lectum (3), love, esteem.

dimitto, -misi, -missum (3), dismiss, adjourn (12) ; give up (76).

dirimo, -remi, -remptum (3), break off.

dirumpo, -rupi, -ruptum (3), break off.

discedo, -cessi, -cessum (3), leave, depart, separate from (75).

discidium, -i, *n.,* separation, division, estrangement.

discindo (3), rend apart.

disco, didici (3), learn.

discordia, -ae, *f.,* discord, quarrel ; hate (24).

disiunctio, -ionis, *f.,* separation.

disiungo, -nxi, -nctum (3), separate, alienate.

dispar, -paris, dissimilar, unequal.

disputatio, -ionis, *f.,* discussion, discourse, treatise.

disputo (1), discuss, argue ; maintain (4) ; state as an opinion (16).

dissensio, -ionis, *f.,* disagreement, enmity.

dissentio, -sensi, -sensum (4), differ, disagree.

dissero, -serui, -sertum (3), discuss, expound (4) ; argue, maintain (13).

dissideo, -sedi, -sessum (2), differ, be at variance.

dissimilitudo, -inis, *f.,* difference, dissimilarity.

dissipo (1), scatter.

dissocio (1), sever.

dissolvo, -solvi, -solutum (3), separate, dissolve.

dissuadeo, -suasi, -suasum (2), speak against.

dissuo (3), unsew.

distantia, -ae, *f.,* unlikeness, divergence.

diu (diutius, diutissime), *adv.,* for a long time.

diutinus, -a, -um, long-continued.

dives, divitis, rich.

divinus, -a, -um, divine, godlike.

divitiae, -arum, *f. pl.,* riches.

do, dedi, datum (1), give ; manus dare, give in, surrender (99) ; operam dare, take pains, see to it (78).

doctus, -a, -um, learned ; *as noun,* scholar, philosopher.

doctrina, -ae, *f.,* learning.

doleo (2), grieve, feel pain ; be distressed at +*dat.* (47, 90).

dolor, -oris, *m.,* grief, pain (22) ; distress (48).

domus, -us, *f.,* house ; *loc.* **domi,** at home.

donum, -i, *n.,* gift.

dubitatio, -ionis, *f.,* doubt, hesitation.

dubito (1), doubt, hesitate.

duco (3), lead ; think, consider (7, 70).

dulcis, -e, pleasant, agreeable, delightful.

dum, *conj.,* while, until.

dumtaxat, *adv.,* merely, only.

duo, -ae, -o, two.

durus, -a, -um, hard.

dux, ducis, leader, guide (19).

e, *see* **ex.**

edo, esse, edi, esum, eat.

educo (1), bring up, educate.

effero, -ferre, extuli, elatum, carry away ; *in pass.,* be carried away, elated ; raise up (100) ; extol (24).

efficio, -ere, -feci, -fectum, accomplish, bring about (59) ; make (54, 81).

effloresco, -ui (3), blossom forth.

egeo (2), +*abl.,* be in need of, need ; **egentes,** the needy.

ego, *pers. pron.,* I ; **egomet,** I myself.

egregius, -a, -um, splendid, distinguished.

eius modi, of that kind, such.

elevo (1), lighten, remove.

eligo, -legi, -lectum (3), choose, select.

eluceo, -xi (2), shine out *or* forth.

eluo, -ui, -utum (3), (wash away), wipe out.

emendatus, -a, -um, faultless.

emitto, -misi, -missum (3), send forth, let out.

emungo, -nxi, -nctum (3), (wipe the nose), befool.

enim, *conj.,* for.

enitor, -nixus (3), strive.

eo, *adv.,* =the *(with comparatives).*

eo, ire, ii, itum, go.

eodem, *adv.,* to the same thing, besides.

equidem, *adv.,* certainly, at all events, indeed.

equus, -i, *m.,* horse.

erga, *prep. with acc.,* towards *(in relations other than motion).*

ergo, *conj.,* therefore.

eripio, -ere, -ripui, -reptum, snatch *or* take away.

erro (1), wander, be mistaken (84).

error, -oris, *m.,* mistake, delusion.

erudio (4), teach, instruct ; **eruditi, -orum,** *m. pl.,* learned men.

erumpo, -rupi, -₁uptum (3), break out.

et, *conj.,* and, also, too ; **et . . . et, -que . . . et,** both . . . and.

etenim, *conj.,* for indeed.

etiam, *adv.,* even, also ; **etiamnunc,** even now.

evenio, -veni, -ventum (4), happen, turn out.

eventus, -us, *m.,* issue, result ; fate (14).

everto, -verti, -versum (3), overthrow.

evidens, -ntis, evident, clear.

evito (1), avoid, shun.

evolo (1), fly forth.

evomo, -ui, -itum (3), disgorge.

ex, *prep. with abl.,* out of, from, of ; in accordance with ; **ex aliqua parte,** to some extent, partly (63, 86).

exaequo (1), put on an equal footing.

exardesco, -arsi, -arsum (3), blaze out, be kindled.

excedo, -cessi, -cessum (3), go out, leave ; **excedere e vita,** to die.

excellens, -ntis, excellent, superior, pre-eminent.

excellentia, -ae, *f.,* excellence, *(personal)* superiority.

excello, -ui, -celsum (3), excel, be excellent.

exceptio, -ionis, *f.,* exception.

excido, -cidi (3), (fall away), be lost.

excipio, -ere, -cepi, -ceptum, (take out) ; except (20, 104).

excito (1), arouse, excite.

excludo, -si, -sum (3), shut out.

excors, -cordis, foolish, senseless.

excusatio, -ionis, *f.,* excuse, defence, plea (43).

exemplar, -aris, *n.,* pattern, likeness (23).

exemplum, -i, *n.,* example, precedent.

exeo, -ire, -ii, -itum, go out, leave, depart.

exercitatio, -ionis, *f.,* practice, training.

exigo, -egi, -actum (3), exact, demand.

exigue, *adv.,* meanly.

exiliter, *adv.,* pettily.

eximo, -emi, -emptum (3), take away.

existimo (1), think, consider.

exitium, -i, *n.,* destruction.

exorior, -ortus (4), arise.

expedit *(impersonal* from **expedio** (4)), it is expedient.

expeditus, -a, -um, rapid.

expello, -puli, -pulsum (3), drive out, expel.

experior, -pertus (4), try, experience, test.

expers, -rtis, without share in.

expeto, -petivi, -petitum (3), seek for, desire.

expleo, -evi, -etum (2), fulfil.

exploro (1), investigate ; *perf. part. pass.,* **exploratus,** certain, sure.

expono, -posui, -positum (3), set forth, state.

exprobro (1), reproach, utter a reproach.

exsilium, -i, *n.,* exile, banishment.

exsisto, -stiti, (3), arise, come into existence ; be displayed (24).

exspecto (1), expect, wait for.

exstinguo, -nxi, -nctum (3), extinguish, destroy ; in *pass.,* die out (78).

exstirpo (1), root out.

exsulo (1), go into exile.

extollo (3), raise.

extremus, -a, -um, last ; *as neuter noun,* the last part, conclusion ; **ad extremum,** at last.

fabula, -ae, *f.,* story, play (24, 75) ; legend (70, 100).

facetus, -a, -um, witty, amusing.

facile, *adv.,* easily, with ease.

facilis, -e, easy, affable.

facilitas, -tatis, *f.,* affability, good nature.

facio, -ere, feci, factum, make, do ; value (37, 56) ; act (9).

factum, -i, *n.,* deed, fact.

facultas, -tatis, *f.,* power, ability (17) ; *in. pl.,* resources.

faeneror (1), put out at interest.

fallax, -acis, false, deceptive ; disappointing (68).

falsus, -a, -um, false, deceitful.

fama, -ae, *f.,* fame, report, reputation (61).

familia, -ae, *f.,* family.

familiaris, -e, intimate, friendly; *as noun,* intimate friend.

familiaritas, -tatis, *f.,* intimacy, friendship.

familiariter, *adv.,* on intimate terms.

famulatus, -us, *m.,* servitude.

famulus, -i, *m.,* servant.

fas, *n.,* *indecl.,* proper, right, lawful.

fastidium, -i, *n.,* pride.

fateor, fassus (2), confess, plead.

fatum, -i, *n.,* fate.

fax, facis, *f.,* torch, firebrand.

felicitas, -tatis, *f.,* good luck, happiness.

felix, -icis, fortunate.

fera, -ae, *f.,* wild beast.

fere, *adv.,* just about, usually, almost.

fero, ferre, tuli, latum, carry, bear, bring forward ; give (56) ; report, say (6, 24) ; *often* = endure ; **ferre legem** (96), bring forward, pass a law ; *in pass.,* be carried to ruin (89).

ferreus, -a, -um, like iron (48) ; hard-hearted (87).

ferus, -a, -um, wild.

fictus, -a, -um, feigned, fictitious (26), false.

fidelis, -e, faithful.

fidelitas, -tatis, *f.,* fidelity, loyalty.

fides, -ei, *f.,* faith (52) ; loyalty (65, 89).

fiducia, -ae, *f.,* confidence.

fidus, -a, -um, faithful, sure.

filius, -i, *m.,* son.

filum, -i, *n.,* (thread) ; style.

fingo, -nxi, fictum (3), feign, form (51), invent (18) ; **res ficta** (24), fiction.

finis,-is, *m.,* end, limit, definition.

fio, fieri, factus sum, be made, become, happen.

firmamentum, -i, *n.,* firm foundation.

firmitas, -tatis, *f.,* firmness (46) ; constancy (19), steadfastness.

firmo (1), strengthen, confirm.

firmus, -a, -um, firm, steadfast, staunch.

flagitiosus, -a, -um, shameful, profligate ; **res flagitiosae,** profligacy (47).

flexibilis, -e, flexible.

floreo (2), prosper.

fons, -ntis, *m.,* fountain, source.

fore, *future infinitive of* **sum.**

fortasse, *adv.,* perhaps.

forte, *adv.,* by chance.

fortis, -e, brave.

fortitudo, -inis, *f.,* courage, bravery.

fortuna, -ae, *f.,* fortune, chance.

fortunatus, -a, -um, fortunate, lucky.

forum, -i, *n.,* the Forum.

fragilis, -e, frail.

frango, fregi, fractum (3), break; *perf. part. pass.,* **fractus** (broken), weak, feeble.

frater, -tris, *m.,* brother.

fraus, fraudis, *f.,* deceit.

frequentia, -ae, *f.,* crowd, gathering.

frons, -ntis, *f.,* brow; expression, look (65).

fructuosus, -a, -um, profitable.

fructus, -us, *m.,* fruit (68); profit (22, 31, 79); enjoyment (87).

fruor, fructus (fruitus), *+abl.,* enjoy.

fucatus, -a, -um, falsified, counterfeit.

fugio, -ere, fugi, fugitum, flee; flee from, shun, avoid.

funditus, *adv.,* entirely, completely.

fungor, functus (3), *+abl.,* perform.

funus, -eris, *n.,* funeral, death.

furor, -oris, *m.,* violence.

futurus, -a, -um, future.

gaudeo, gavisus (2), rejoice; *+abl.* (82, 90).

gener, -eri, *m.,* son-in-law.

generosus, -a, -um, noble (29).

genus, -eris, *n.,* race, family (70); kind (48); class, sort (15, 62, 79); manner (12).

gero, gessi, gestum (3), carry on, conduct; **se gerere,** behave.

gigno, genui, genitum (3), beget, produce; give rise to (20).

gloria, -ae, *f.,* glory, fame; reputation (5).

gloriosus, -a, -um, boastful, braggart.

gradus, -us, *m.,* rank, station (12).

Graecia, -ae, *f.,* Greece.

Graecus, -a, -um, Greek; *as noun,* a Greek.

grates, *only nom. and acc. pl., f.,* thanks.

gratia, -ae, *f.,* gratitude, repayment (31); recompense (53); **gratias agere,** thank.

gratus, -a, -um, pleasant, pleasing, welcome.

gravis, -e, severe, heavy; burdensome (11); severe, firm (64, 99); respectable (95), dignified (32).

gravitas, -tatis, *f.,* (weight), seriousness (4, 66).

graviter, *adv.,* seriously, grievously; with dignity (77).

gravor (1), (be vexed), be unwilling (17).

grex, gregis, *m.,* flock, set.

habena, -ae, *f.,* rein.

habeo (2), have, hold, consider; afford (27); involve (38); **sermonem habere,** deliver a discourse; **diligentiam habere,** take care.

hactenus, *adv.,* up to this point, thus far.

haud, not; **haud scio an,** I rather think.

haudquaquam, *adv.,* by no means.

hemicyclium, -i, *n.*, recess (*semicircular in shape, with seats*), summer-house.

herba, -ae, *f.*, green shoot.

hercle, *interj.*, by Hercules!

hic, haec, hoc, *demonstrative pronoun*, this; this latter (20, 90).

hic, *adv.*, here.

hodie, *adv.*, today.

homo, -inis, *m. and f.*, human being, man.

honestas, -tatis, *f.*, honour, integrity.

honeste, *adv.*, with honour *or* integrity.

honestus, -a, -um, honourable.

honor(s), honoris, *m.*, honour, respect (23, 78); public office (*frequently*).

hortor (1), exhort, persuade.

hortus, -i, *m.*, garden; *in pl.*, park, grounds.

hospes, -itis, *m.*, guest-friend.

hostis, -is, *m.*, enemy.

huc, *adv.*, to this, hither.

humanitas, -tatis, *f.*, kindliness (8); sympathy (48).

humanus, -a, -um, human.

humilis, -e, mean (24); humble (70).

iaceo (2), lie, be prostrate (59).

iam, *adv.*, now, already.

iamdudum, *adv.*, for some time.

idcirco, *adv.*, therefore, on that account.

idem, eadem, idem, the same, he too.

idoneus, -a, -um, suitable, fitted.

igitur, therefore.

ignarus, -a, -um, ignorant, not knowing.

ignavia, -ae, *f.*, cowardice.

ignis, -is, *m.*, fire.

ignoratio, -ionis, *f.*, ignorance.

ignoro (1), not to know.

ignosco, -novi, -notum (3), +*dat.*, pardon.

ille, -a, illud, *demonstrative pronoun*, that; he, she, it; the former (63, 90).

illudo, -si, -sum (3), deceive, dupe.

illustris, -e, illustrious, famous, renowned.

illustro (1), make clear, explain.

imago, -inis, *f.*, image, likeness.

imbecillitas, -tatis, *f.*, weakness.

imbecillus, -a, -um, weak.

imbellis, -e, cowardly; res imbelles, cowardice.

imitor (1), imitate.

immanitas, -tatis, *f.*, churlishness, barbarism.

immortalis, -e, immortal.

immortalitas, -tatis, *f.*, immortality.

immunis, -e, selfish.

immuto (1), change, transform.

impedio (4), hinder, prevent.

impello, -puli, -pulsum (3), drive.

impendeo (2), +*dat.*, hang over, threaten.

imperator, -oris, *m.*, commander-in-chief.

imperitus, -a, -um, unskilful, ignorant.

imperium, -i, *n.*, military command, empire (28).

impero (1), order, bid; +*dat.*, control, master.

impertio (4), impart.

impetro (1), obtain.

impetus, -us, *m.*, onset, impulse.

impietas, -tatis, *f.*, disloyalty, treason.

implico (1), involve.

importunitas, -tatis, *f.*, insolence.

improbus, -a, -um, wicked.

improvidus, short-sighted, imprudent.

impudenter, *adv.*, shamelessly.

impurus, -a, -um, sordid, abandoned, vile.

in, *prep. with acc.*, to, into ; *with abl.*, in, on, upon, in the case of.

inanimus, -a, -um, inanimate.

inanis, -e, empty, vain, worthless.

incertus, -a, -um, uncertain, unsure.

incido, -cidi (3), fall into (34, 42), happen ; chance to talk of (2).

incipio, -ere, -cepi, -ceptum, begin.

incommodum, -i, *n.*, trouble, misfortune.

incommodus, -a, -um, inconvenient, troublesome, disagreeable.

incommode, *adv.*, disagreeably.

incredibilis, -e, incredible.

incultus, -a, -um, unadorned.

incuria, -ae, *f.*, want of care, neglect.

indico (1), indicate, show.

indigens, -ntis, +*gen.*, in want of.

indigentia, -ae, *f.*, want, need.

indigeo (2), +*gen.*, need.

indignus, -a, -um, unworthy ; +*abl.*, unworthy of.

induco, -xi, -ctum (3), introduce (3) ; induce (59).

indulgeo, -ulsi, -ultum (2), give oneself up to (54) ; +*dat.*, be indulgent to.

ineo, -ire, -ii, -itum, enter ; ineuntis aetatis (33), of the early days of life ; ineunte aetate (74), in boyhood.

infamia, -ae, *f.*, discredit, disgrace.

infero, -ferre, -tuli, illatum, bring against ; wage against (43).

inferi, -orum, *m. pl.*, those below, the shades.

inferior, -ius, lower, inferior (69) ; virtute inferiores (7), inferior to, *i.e.* not as important as virtue.

infidus, -a, -um, disloyal, false.

infinitus, -a, -um, unlimited, boundless.

infirmitas, -tatis, *f.*, weakness.

infirmus, -a, -um, weak.

inflammo (1), inflame.

influo, -uxi, -uxum (3), (flow into) ; steal, insinuate oneself (96).

ingenium, -i, *n.*, character (65, 74) ; intellect (70).

ingens, -ntis, vast, great, huge.

ingenuus, -a, -um, open, sincere, frank.

ingratus, -a, -um, ungrateful.

ingravesco (3), grow heavy *or* burdensome.

inhumane, *adv.*, more heartlessly, with less kindness.

inhumanus, -a, -um, unkind, unfeeling.

inimicitia, -ae, *f.*, enmity, quarrel.

inimicus, -a, -um, unfriendly, hostile ; *as noun*, (personal) enemy.

initium, -i, *n.*, beginning.

iniuria, -ae, *f.*, wrong-doing, violence (35) ; injustice (42).

iniustus, -a, -um, unjust ; res iniustae, injustice.

inopia, -ae, *f.*, poverty, want, need.

inops, -opis, poor; +*gen.*, poor in.

inquam, -is, -it, say.

insector (1), rail at, inveigh against.

insignis, -e, conspicuous.

insinuo (1), insinuate, ingratiate (oneself).

insipiens, -ntis, foolish ; *as a noun*, fool.

instituo, -ui, -utum (3), begin.

institutum, -i, *n.*, doctrine, principle.

insuavis, -e, unpleasant, disagreeable.

insum, -esse, -fui, be in *or* included.

integritas, -tatis, *f.*, integrity, uprightness.

intellego, -exi, -ectum (3), understand, perceive.

intemperatus, -a, -um, immoderate, excessive.

intempestivus, -a, -um, untimely, ill-timed.

inter, *prep. with acc.*, between, among.

intercedo, -cessi, -cessum (3), intervene.

interdum, *adv.*, sometimes.

intereo, -ire, -ii, -itum, perish.

interitus, -us, *m.*, death, ruin, destruction.

intermissio, -ionis, *f.*, interruption, discontinuance.

internosco, -novi, -notum (3), distinguish.

interpono, -posui, -positum (3), insert.

interpretor (1), understand to be, interpret (21).

intersum, -esse, -fui, be between; *impersonally*, there is a difference (48, 95).

intolerabilis, -e, unbearable, insufferable.

intractatus, -a, -um, untamed ; *of a horse*, wild, unbroken.

introeo, -ire, -ii, -itum, go in, enter.

intueor (2), gaze upon, look at.

invehor, -vectus (3), attack, inveigh against.

invenio, -veni, -ventum (4), come upon, find.

inveteratus, -a, -um, old, of long standing.

invideo, -vidi, -visum (2), envy, feel envy.

invidia, -ae, *f.*, odium, unpopularity.

invidiosus, -a, -um, exciting envy, unpopular.

invidus, -a, -um, envious.

invito (1), invite.

invitus, -a, -um, unwilling.

ipse, -a, -um, self ; very.

is, ea, id, *demonstrative pronoun*, that; he, she, it; iste, -a, -ud, *demonstrative pronoun*, that (*of yours*) ; that you talk of, *etc.*

istuc, *neut. sing.* of istic=iste.

ita, *adv.*, so, in such a way ; on the condition that (1).

Italia, -ae, *f.*, Italy.

itaque, *conj.*, and so, therefore.

item, *adv.*, likewise, so, in like manner.

iter, itineris, *n.*, a going, journey.

iterum, *adv.*, a second time, again.

iucunde, *adv.*, in a pleasant manner.

iucunditas, -tatis, *f.*, cheerfulness, joy.

iucundus, -a, -um, pleasant, delightful.

iudicium, -i, *n.*, judgment, examination.

iudico (1), judge, consider, decide upon (74) ; form judgment (85).

iungo, -nxi, -nctum (3), join, unite.

iurgium, -i, *n.*, quarrel.

ius, iuris, *n.*, right ; claim (63) ; meo iure, in my own right, *i.e.* as I have a right to do ; ius civile, civil law (6).

ius iurandum, iuris iurandi, *n.*, oath.

iustus, -a, -um, just, fair.

iuvo, iuvi, iutum (1), help, assist ; *impersonally*, it pleases, delights.

labefacto (1), shake, overthrow.

labes, -is, *f.*, ruin.

labor, -oris, *m.*, toil.

labor, lapsus (3), fall, rush down.

laboro (1), labour, toil.

lacrima, -ae, *f.*, tear.

laetor (1), rejoice, exult.

laetus, -a, -um, glad, joyful.

Latini, -orum, *m.*, Latins.

latus, -eris, *n.*, side.

laudabilis, -e, worthy of praise, laudable.

laudo (1), praise, extol.

laus, laudis, *f.*, praise ; *in pl.*, merits (98).

laute, *adv.*, splendidly, finely.

laxus, -a, -um, loose.

lego, legi, lectum (3), read.

levis, -e, light (22) ; fickle, worthless.

levitas, -tatis, *f.*, fickleness, inconstancy ; folly (93).

levo (1), lighten, relieve of.

lex, legis, *f.*, law.

libenter, *adv.*, with pleasure (96), readily (68).

liber, -era, -erum, free ; *as noun*, a free man (89).

liber, -bri, *m.*, book.

liberalis, -e, liberal, generous.

liberalitas, -tatis, *f.*, liberality, generosity.

liberaliter, *adv.*, like a free man.

libere, *adv.*, freely, candidly.

libero (1), set free.

libet (2), *impersonal*, it pleases ; mihi libet, I am minded.

libido, -inis, *f.*, lust (19, 83) ; licentiousness.

licentia, -ae, *f.*, licence.

licet (2), *impersonal*, it is lawful, one may ; *as conj.*, + *subj.*, although.

litigo (1), quarrel.

loco (1), place ; rank (104).

locus, -i, *m.*, place (22) ; position (40) ; birth, rank (94) ; room (52, 97) ; case (47) ; subject, topic (46) ; *in pl.*, the country (68).

longe, *adv.*, afar, far, a long way ; by far, far, greatly ; *comp.*, longius, further.

loquor, locutus (3), speak, say.

lubenter, *see* libenter.

lumen, -inis, *n.*, light

maereo (2), grieve, grieve for.

maeror, -oris, *m.*, grief, sadness.

maestitia, -ae, *f.*, sadness, grief, sorrow.

magis, *adv.*, more.

magistratus, -us, *m.*, magistracy.

magnificentia, -ae, *f.*, magnificence, pomp.

magnificus, -a, -um, grand, magnificent.

magnitudo, inis, *f.*, greatness, size ; great amount (29).

magnus, -a, -um, (maior, maximus), great, important.

maiestas, -tatis, *f.*, majesty, dignity.

maiores, -um, *m. pl.*, ancestors.

maledictum, -i, *n.*, abuse.

malitia, -ae, *f.*, ill-will, malice.

malo, malle, malui, prefer, wish rather, choose.

malum, -i, *n.*, evil.

malus, -a, -um, bad, evil ; malae res, misfortune, adversity.

mando (1), entrust, commit.

maneo, mansi, mansum (2), remain, stay.

manus, -us, *f.*, hand ; est in manibus (96), it is in (every one's) hands, it is published ; in manibus habui (102), had within reach.

mater, -tris, *f.*, mother.

maxime, *superl. adv.*, (magnopere), most of all, especially, very greatly.

medicina, -ae, *f.*, medicine, remedy.

mediocris, -e, ordinary (22), mean (61).

medius, -a, -um, middle, mid, midst.

melior, -ius, *comp.* of bonus, better.

memini, -isse, remember.

memorabilis, -e, memorable, worth relating.

memoria, -ae, *f.*, memory, remembrance ; record (38).

memoriter, *adv.*, from memory.

mensis, -is, *m.*, month.

mentio, -ionis, *f.*, mention.

mentior (4), lie, cheat, deceive.

merces, -edis, *f.*, reward.

mereor (2), deserve.

meritum, -i, *n.*, good service, kindness, benefit.

metior (4), measure.

metuo, -ui, -utum (3), fear.

meus, -a, -um, my, mine.

miles, -itis, *m.*, soldier.

militia, -ae, *f.*, military service, service abroad ; militiae, *loc.*, on service, abroad.

minime, *superl. adv.*, least, by no means, not at all.

minimus, -a, -um, *superl. adj.* (parvus), smallest, least.

minister, -tri, *m.,* minister, servant.

minor, -us, (*compar. of* **parvus**), smaller, less; **natu minor** (32), younger.

minus, *compar. adv.,* less, too little; *sometimes* = not.

mirabilis, -e, astonishing.

miror (1), wonder (at), be surprised.

mirus, -a, -um, wonderful, strange, astonishing.

misceo, -cui, mixtum (2), mix, mingle.

moderate, *adv.,* temperately, with moderation.

modestus, -a, -um, self-restrained, sober.

modius, -i, *m.,* corn-measure, peck.

modo, *adv.,* lately (6); just now (15), just; only (70, 93, 97); *as conj.,* +*subj.,* provided that (61).

modus, -i, *m.,* manner, way.

moleste, *adv.,* with **ferre,** be annoyed (at), take ill.

molestia, -ae, *f.,* annoyance, vexation.

molestus, -a, -um, troublesome, annoying.

mollis, -e, unmanly.

moneo (2), warn, advise, admonish.

monitio, -ionis, *f.,* warning, admonition.

montuosus, -a, -um, mountainous.

morior, -i, mortuus, die.

mors, mortis, *f.,* death.

mortalis, -e, mortal.

mortuus, -a, -um, dead.

mos, moris, *m.,* custom, manner; *in pl.,* character.

motus, -us, *m.,* movement, motion; emotion (48).

moveo, movi, motum (2), move, affect, stir (29).

muliercula, -ae, *f., dimin. of* **mulier,** weak woman.

multiplex, -plicis, manifold (88, 92); changeable, unreliable (65).

multitudo, -inis, *f.,* (large) number, the mob (41); ordinary people (50).

multo, *adv.,* much, by far.

multum, *adv.,* much, greatly, very.

multus, -a, -um, much; *in pl.,* many.

mundus, -i, *m.,* the universe.

munio (4), fortify.

munus, -eris, *n.,* duty (7, 22, 67).

muto (1), change.

mutuus, -a, -um, mutual.

nam (namque), for.

nanciscor, nactus *or* **nanctus** (3), get, obtain, find.

nans, nantis, (swimming), living in the water.

narro (1), narrate, tell.

nascor, natus (3), be born, arise, come into existence.

natura, -ae, *f.,* nature; disposition (7).

naturalis, -e, natural.

natus, -i, *m.,* child, son.

natu, *only in abl. sing.,* by birth.

ne, *adv. and conj.,* not, that not, lest; **ne** . . . **quidem,** not even.

-ne, *interrog. enclitic,* whether.

nec, *see* **neque.**

necessarius, -a, -um, necessary ;
  inevitable, indispensable (86);
  closely connected, intimate.
necesse, *neut. adj.*, necessary,
  inevitable.
necessitudo, -inis, *f.*, bond.
neco (1), kill.
nefarius, -a, -um, wicked, im-
  pious.
nefas, *indecl.*, wrong, impiety.
neglegens, -ntis, careless.
neglegentia, -ae, *f.*, carelessness, neglect.
neglego, -exi, -ectum (3), neglect, disregard.
nego (1), deny, say . . . not ;
  say ' no ' (93).
negotium, -i, *n.*, business.
nemo (*gen.* nullius, *abl.* nullo),
  no-one, no man, nobody.
nequaquam, *adv.*, by no means.
neque, *conj.*, nor, and . . . not ;
  neque enim, for indeed . . .
  not ; neque . . . neque, neither
  . . . nor.
nequeo, -ire, -ivi (4), be unable.
nescio, -i(v)i, -itum (4), not
  know ; nescio quo modo *or*
  quo pacto, somehow or other ;
  nescio quis, quem (*lit., I know
  not who*), a certain.
neu *or* neve, *conj.*, and not, nor.
neuter, -tra, -trum, neither
  (of two) ; *in pl.*, neither
  party.
nihil *or* nil, *indecl.*, nothing.
nihilum, -i, *n.*, nothing.
nimirum, *adv.*, doubtless, certainly (23).
nimis, *adv.*, too much, too, very.
nimius, -a, -um, excessive, too
  much.

nisi, *conj.*, if not, unless ;
  except (72, 97).
no (1), swim.
noceo (2), +*dat.*, hurt, damage,
  injure.
nodus, -i, *m.*, knot, bond.
nolo, nolle, nolui, be unwilling,
  not wish.
nomen, -inis, *n.*, name.
nomino (1), name, mention
  (15) ; *in pass.*, take its name
  (26).
non, *adv.*, not.
Nonae, -arum, *f. plur.*, Nones.
nonne, *interrog. particle*, is it
  not?, surely.
non nullus, -a, -um, some,
  several, few.
non numquam, *adv.*, sometimes.
norma, -ae, *f.*, rule, standard.
nos, nostri (nostrum), nobis, we.
nosco, novi, notum (3), *in perf.
  tenses*, know, recognise (79).
nosmet, we ourselves.
noster, -tra, -trum, our.
nota, -ae, *f.*, mark.
noto (1), mark, brand.
notus, -a, -um, known.
novitas, -tatis, *f.*, novelty.
novus, -a, -um, new, novel.
nullus, -a, -um, none, no.
num, *interrog. particle*, surely
  not (36) ; *in indirect question*,
  whether, if (97).
numero (1), count, reckon.
numerus, -i, *m.*, number.
nunc, *adv.*, now.
nunquam, *adv.*, never.
nuper, *adv.*, lately.
nusquam, *adv.*, nowhere.
nutrix, -icis, *f.*, nurse.
nutus, -us, *m.*, nod.

ob, *prep. with acc.*, on account of.
obeo, -ire, -ii, -itum, discharge, perform.
obiurgatio, -ionis, *f.*, reproof.
obiurgo (1), reprove, scold.
oblectatio, -ionis, *f.*, delight, pleasure.
obscuro, (1), conceal, forget.
obscurus, -a, -um, dark, obscure, unintelligible.
obsequium, -i, *n.*, complaisance, obsequiousness.
obsequor, -secutus (3), +*dat.*, obey, gratify.
observo (1), watch (58) ; honour (26).
obsisto, -stiti (3), oppose, resist.
obsurdesco, -surdui (3), (become deaf), turn deaf ear to.
occido, -cidi, -casum (3), perish.
occulto (1), keep hidden, conceal.
occultus, -a, -um, secret.
occupo (1), seize.
oculus, -i, *m.*, eye.
odi, -isse, hate ; *fut. part.* osurus (59), going to hate.
odiosus, -a, -um, hateful, objectionable.
odium, -i, *n.*, hatred, ill-will, animosity.
offendo, -ndi, -nsum (3), offend, annoy.
offensio, -ionis, *f.*, indignation (77) ; offence (88) ; cause of offence (85).
offero, -ferre, obtuli, oblatum, bring up against.
officiose, *adv.*, courteously, kindly.
officium, -i, *n.*, kind service (24, 49, 58, 85) ; duty (8).

omitto, -misi, -missum (3), omit, pass over (64).
omnino, *adv.*, altogether ; speaking generally (74, 78) ; to be sure (69, 98) ; *with negative*, at all.
omnis, -e, every, all.
opera, -ae, *f.*, service, assistance (51) ; operam dare, take pains, give attention to.
opinio, -ionis, *f.*, opinion, belief (30) ; reputation (98).
opinor (1), think, believe.
oportet (2), *impers.*, it is right, it behoves (*with acc. and infin.*) ; *with subj.* (66).
opportunitas, -tatis, *f.*, conveniency, advantage.
opportunus, -a, -um, convenient, suitable.
opprimo, -pressi, -pressum (3), crush, overwhelm.
(ops), opis, *f.*, help ; *in pl.*, wealth, means, resources.
optime, *superl. adv.*, (bene), best, in the best way.
optimus, -a, -um, *superl. of* bonus, best, most excellent.
opto (1), wish, long for.
opulentus, -a, -um, wealthy, rich.
opus, operis, *n.*, work, deed (72) ; need, necessity ; opus est (51) ; it is necessary, expedient.
oraculum, -i, *n.*, oracle.
oratio, -ionis, *f.*, speech, discourse.
orbis, -is, *m.*, (circle), the world.
orbo (1) +*abl.*, deprive *or* bereave of.
ordo, -inis, *m.*, order, rank.

orior, ortus (4), arise, rise, begin, take its origin.

ornamentum, -i, *n.*, adornment, ornament.

ortus, -us, *m.*, origin.

os, oris, *n.*, face, mouth ; voice (86).

ostendo, -di, -sum *or* -tum (3), show.

ostentatio, -ionis, *f.*, showing off, display, ostentation.

otiosus, -a, -um, leisure, at leisure ; free from public cares (86).

ovis, -is, *f.*, sheep.

pactum, -i, *n.*, way, manner ; quo pacto (7), how ; *see also* nescio.

paedagogus, -i, *m.*, tutor.

paene, *adv.*, almost.

par, paris, *n.*, a pair.

par, paris, equal ; right (65), fair (82) ; equal to (69).

parasitus, -i, *m.*, hanger-on, parasite.

paratus, -a, -um, ready, prepared.

parens, -ntis, parent.

pareo (2), + *dat.*, obey.

pario, -ere, peperi, partum, beget, produce, create, obtain (51).

pariter, *adv.*, equally, exactly.

paro (1), prepare ; obtain, procure.

pars, partis, *f.*, part, some ; partes (77), a party ; ex aliqua parte (63, 86), in some degree, to some extent ; ex omni parte (79), in every respect ; ex altera parte (63),

... on the one side ... on the other.

partim, *adv.*, partly.

partior (4), share, take a part in.

parturio (4), be in travail.

parum, *adv.*, too little, not ; not enough (18).

parumper, *adv.*, for a short time.

parvus, -a, -um, small, little.

pastor, -oris, *m.*, shepherd.

patefacio, -ere, -feci, -factum, open, make plain.

pateo (2), lie open (13) ; is free, allowed (83).

pater, -tris, *m.*, father ; patres *or* patres conscripti, the Senate.

patienter, *adv.*, patiently.

patior, -i, passus, suffer, allow.

patria, -ae, *f.*, native-land, fatherland, country.

patronus, i, *m.*, patron ; advocate, defender (25).

paucus, -a, -um, *in pl.*, few.

paulo, *adv.*, (by) a little, (*chiefly with comparatives*).

paulum, *adv.*, a little, somewhat.

pax, pacis, *f.*, peace.

peccatum, -i, *n.*, sin, error.

pecco (1), do wrong, sin, err.

pectus, -oris, *n.*, breast, heart.

pecunia, -ae, *f.*, money ; sum of money (63).

pecus, -udis, *f.*, beast, animal.

pello, pepuli, pulsum (3), drive out.

penuria, -ae, *f.*, dearth, scarcity.

per, *prep. with acc.*, through ; by means of, by .

percipio, -ere, -cepi, -ceptum, perceive, observe (23) ; obtain (26).

perduco, **-xi**, -ctum (3), continue (34) ; guide (73).

peregrinatio, -ionis, *f.*, a foreign tour.

peregrinus, **-a**, **-um**, foreigner, stranger.

perfectus, **-a**, **-um**, faultless, full-grown (9) ; perfect.

pergo, perrexi, perrectum (3), go on, proceed.

pergratus, -a, -um, very pleasant *or* welcome.

periclitor (1), test.

periculum, -i, *n.*, danger, risk.

permaneo, -mansi, -mansum (2), remain, continue.

permultus, -a, -um, very many.

pernicies, -ei, *f.*, destruction.

perniciosus,-a,-um, mischievous.

perpendo, -ndi, -nsum (3), weigh carefully, value.

persaepe, *adv.*, very often.

persequor, -secutus (3), pursue, prove (45).

persevero (1), persist, maintain.

Persicus, -a, -um, Persian.

persolvo, -vi, -solutum (3), pay fully.

persona, -ae, *f.*, character (*in a play*).

perspicio, -ere, -spexi, -spectum, perceive.

perstringo, -nxi, -ictum (3), touch upon, treat briefly.

perterreo (2), frighten thoroughly.

pertineo, -ui, -tentum (2), pertain, concern.

pervenio, -veni, -ventum (4), come to, arrive, reach.

perverse, *adv.*, perversely, wrongly.

pestis, -is, *f.*, pest, plague ; bane (91).

peto, petivi, petitum (3), seek, ask.

pietas, -tatis, *f.*, filial affection (11), piety.

pila, -ae, *f.*, ball, ball-game.

pinguis, -e, fat ; stupid.

placeo (2), +*dat.*, please ; *im-person.*, it pleases.

plane, *adv.*, entirely, utterly.

plaudo, -si, -sum (3), applaud, clap.

plebs, plebis, *f.*, the people, the plebs.

plecto (3), *only in pass.*, suffer, be punished.

plenus, -a, -um, full.

plerique, -aeque, -aque, the majority, most.

plerumque, *adv.*, for the most part, generally, often.

plurimum, *adv.*, most, very much ; plurimum posse (55), to be most influential ; plurimum confidere (30), to have most confidence.

plus, pluris, *in sing. neut. only*, more ; *pl.*, plures, plura, more, several ; many (45) ; *superl.*, plurimus, -a, -um, most.

poena, -ae, *f.*, penalty (37) ; punishment (41).

pono, posui, positum (3), place, lay aside (33) ; *in pass.*, depend *or* rely on (4, 7, 20, 30).

pontifex, -ficis, *m.*, a priest, pontifex.

popularis, -is, a demagogue (95) ; *as adj.*, popular (96).

populus, -i, *m.*, people, nation.

possessio, -ionis, *f.*, possession, tenure.

possum, posse, potui, be able, can.

post, *prep. with acc.*, after, behind ; *as adv.*, afterwards, later.

posteritas, -tatis, *f.*, posterity.

posterus, -a, -um, coming after ; posteri, -orum, posterity (102) ; in posterum, for the future (23).

postremo, *adv.*, lastly (86) ; in fine (93).

postulatio, -ionis, *f.*, demand, claim.

postulo (1), demand, claim.

potens, -ntis, powerful.

potentia, -ae, *f.*, power, influence.

potestas, -tatis, *f.*, power (62, 87) ; position of authority (63) ; office (54).

potior, -ius, preferable, better.

potissimum, *adv.*, especially, in preference to all others.

potius, *compar. adv.*, rather.

praebeo (2), offer, make.

praeceps, -ipitis, headlong.

praeceptum, -i, *n.*, precept, rule.

praecipio, -ere, -cepi, -ceptum, enjoin (60) ; inculcate (75).

praeclare, *adv.*, splendidly, wonderfully.

praeclarus, -a, -um, splendid.

praecurro, -curri, -cursum (3), outstrip, outrun.

praeditus, -a, -um, +*abl.*, endowed with, possessed of.

praefero, -ferre, -tuli, -latum, prefer.

praeluceo, -uxi (2), (shine before), light up (23).

praepono, -posui, -positum (3), prefer.

praeposterus, -a, -um, in reverse order.

praepotens, -ntis, very powerful.

praesagio (4), have a presentiment of.

praesens, -ntis, present.

praesertim, *adv.*, especially.

praesidium, -i, *n.*, protection, defence.

praestabilis, -e, excellent.

praestans, -ntis, pre-eminent, superior, excellent.

praestantia, -ae, *f.*, pre-eminence, superiority, excellence.

praesto, -stiti, -stitum (1), +*dat.*, be superior (19, 23) ; *trans.*, show, display (64).

praesto, *adv.*, at hand, ready.

praesum, -esse, -fui, +*dat.*, be at the head of ; direct.

praeter, *prep. with acc.*, beyond (4), except.

praeterea, *adv.*, besides.

praetereo, -ire, -ii, -itum, pass by, overlook.

praetextus, -a, -um, bordered ; toga praetexta, toga bordered with purple.

praetor, -oris, *m.*, praetor.

precor (1), pray, entreat, beseech.

pretiosus, -a, -um, precious, costly.

pridie, *adv.*, the day before.

primo, *adv.*, at first.

primus, -a, -um, first.

primum, *adv.*, in the first instance.

princeps, -ipis, first, of primary importance (26).

principium, -i, *n.,* beginning ; principio, in the first place.

prius, *adv.,* before, sooner ; first (15, 59).

privatus, -a, -um, private.

pro, *prep. with abl.,* on behalf of, for.

pro, *interj.,* Oh! Ah!

probitas, -tatis, *f.,* honesty, uprightness, integrity.

probo (1), approve of.

proclivis, -e, (downhill), headlong (41) ; inclined (66).

procul, *adv.,* far off.

prodo, -didi, -ditum (3), hand down.

profecto, *adv.,* certainly, assuredly.

proficiscor, profectus (3), start ; originate from (29, 30, 51).

profiteor, -fessus (2), profess.

profugio, -ere, -fugi, run away, escape.

progredior, -i, -gressus, advance, proceed.

prope, *adv.,* near, nearly, almost.

propensus, -a, -um, inclined *or* disposed to.

propinquitas, -tatis, *f.,* (nearness), relationship.

propinquus, -a, -um, near, related ; *as a noun,* relative (19, 41, 70).

propono, -posui, -positum (3), put forward, propose (63) ; set before oneself (102).

proprium, -i, *n.,* the characteristic, special attribute.

propter, *prep. with acc.,* by reason of, on account of ; because of (41).

propterea, *adv.,* on this (that) account.

prorsus, *adv.,* entirely, absolutely.

prosequor, -secutus (3), attend upon.

prosperus, -a, -um, prosperous.

prospicio, -ere, -spexi, -spectum, foresee.

prosum, prodesse, profui, + *dat.,* benefit.

proveho, -vexi, -vectum (3), carry forward ; *in pass.,* advance.

proverbium, -i, *n.,* proverb.

provideo, -vidi, -visum (2), foresee.

provisio, -ionis, *f.,* provision, safeguard.

proxime, *superl. adv.,* (prope), nearest.

proximus, -a, -um, nearest, last, (7) ; *as noun,* next of kin, near relation.

prudens, -ntis, experienced, practised (6) ; sagacious, wise (5).

prudenter, *adv.,* skilfully (1), wisely (6).

prudentia, -ae, *f.,* skill, professional learning.

publicus, -a, -um, public.

puer, -eri, *m.,* boy.

pulcher, -chra, -chrum, beautiful, noble ; lovely (80).

pulchritudo, -inis, *f.,* beauty.

puto (1), think, consider, believe.

quaero, quaesivi, quaesitum (3), seek, look for (65), ask, question ; examine (7).

quaestio, -ionis, *f.*, question (65) ; court of enquiry (37).

qualis, -e, *correl.*, such as, as ; talis . . . qualis, such . . . as.

qualis, -e, *interrog.*, of what kind ? *in exclam.*, what a (25).

quam, *adv. and conj.*, how ; than (*after comparat.*) ; *with superl. adj. or adv.*, as . . . as possible ; pridie quam (12), the day before . . .

quam ob rem, wherefore.

quamquam, *conj.*, although ; and yet.

quamvis, *adv., and conj.*, although ; however (17, 35, 73) ; quamvis multi (91), as many as you choose.

quando, *conj.*, when? ; *adv.*, at any time (*after si, ne, num*).

quantus, -a, -um, how much? how great? ; *correl.*, as much as ; tantus . . . quantus, as much . . . as ; quantum (19), as far as.

quapropter, *adv.*, wherefore.

qua re, *adv.*, wherefore.

quasi, *adv.*, as though ; *with single words*, a sort of, as one might say.

quatenus, *adv.*, how far (36) ; *rel.*, to which extent (61).

quattuor, four.

-que, *enclitic conj.*, and.

quem ad modum, how? (41) ; *relat.*, as, just as.

queo, -ire (4), be able, can.

querella, -ae, *f.*, regret (2) ; complaint (35).

queror, questus (3), complain.

qui, quae, quod, *rel. pron.*, who, which, what.

qui, quae, quod, *interrog. adj.*, which? what?

qui, quae (qua), quod, *indefin. adj.*, any (61, 70).

qui, *adv.* (*old abl. of* qui), how? in what way?

quia, *conj.*, because.

qui-, quae-, quodcunque, whoever, whatever.

quid (*neut. of* quis), *adv.*, why?

quidam, quaedam, quoddam, a certain, a certain one, one.

quidem, *adv.*, indeed ; ne ... quidem, not even.

quies, quietis, *f.*, rest, sleep.

quin, *conj.*, but that, that not, who not (68) ; *as adv.*, nay more, moreover (59, 68, 87).

quinquennium, -i, *n.*, period of five years.

quintum, *adv.*, for the fifth time.

quippe, *conj.*, for, since ; quippe qui, inasmuch as.

quis, quid, *interrog. pron.*, who?, which?, what?

quis, qua, quid, *indef. pron.*, anyone, anything.

quisnam, quaenam, quidnam, who then? who, pray?

quispiam, quaepiam, quidpiam, any one, anything.

quisquam, quidquam *or* quicquam, any, any one, any thing.

quisque, quaeque, quidque (*adj.*, quodque), each, every, a man.

quisquis, quicquid (quidquid), whoever, whatever.

quivis, quaevis, quidvis, (whom you please), anyone, anything (35, 73).

quo, *adv.*, whither, to which.

quo, *conj.*, *used with compar.*, in order that.

quoad, *conj.*, as long as.

quocirca, *adv.*, wherefore, on which account.

quod, *conj.*, because, that, whereas (90) ; **quod si**, but if.

quomodo, *adv.*, in what way? how?

quondam, *adv.*, formerly, at times.

quoniam, *conj.*, since.

quoque, *adv.*, also, too.

quoquo, *adv.*, whithersoever (22).

quorsum, *adv.*, whither? to what end?

quot, *indecl.*, how many?

rapax, **-acis**, greedy.

rarus, **-a**, **-um**, rare.

ratio, **-ionis**, *f.*, reason (89), method (26), mode (87) ; terms (101) ; theory (52) ; balance (58).

reapse, *adv.*, really, in reality.

recens, **-ntis**, recent.

recipio, **-ere**, **-cepi**, **-ceptum**, receive, accept.

recordatio, **-ionis**, *f.*, recollection.

recte, *adv.*, rightly.

rectus, **-a**, **-um**, right.

recuso (1), refuse.

redamo (1), love in return.

reddo, **-didi**, **-ditum** (3), return, repay, pay out (58).

redeo, **-ire**, **-ii**, **-itum**, return.

reditus, **-us**, *m.*, a return.

reduco, **-xi**, **-ctum** (3), lead back, escort home (12).

redundo (1), overflow, spread (76).

refero, **-ferre**, **rettuli**, **relatum**, refer (32) ; make recompense (53).

refert, *impers.*, it matters ; **quid refert** (26), what does it matter?

reficio, **-ere**, **-feci**, **-fectum**, re-elect.

regno (1), have royal power, reign.

regnum, **-i**, *n.*, royal power.

religio, **-ionis**, *f.*, reverence.

religiosus, **-a**, **-um**, pious, reverential (13).

reliquus, **-a**, **-um**, remaining, left ; *in plur.*, the rest.

remissio, **-ionis**, *f.*, relaxation.

remissus, **-a**, **-um**, (relaxed), genial, gay (66).

remitto, **-misi**, **-missum**, slacken.

removeo, **-movi**, **-motum** (2), remove, withdraw.

remuneratio, **-ionis**, *f.*, return, repayment.

repello, **reppuli**, **repulsum** (3), repel, repudiate.

repente, *adv.*, suddenly.

reperio, **repperi**, **repertum** (4), find.

reposco (3), demand back.

reprehendo, **-ndi**, **-nsum** (3), take hold of ; censure (59).

repudio (1), renounce (47, 48) ; reject (68, 96).

repugnanter, *adv.*, unwillingly, with reluctance.

repugno (1), be inimical *or* contrary to.

requies, **-etis**, *f.*, repose, rest.

requiro, **-quisivi**, **-quisitum** (3), seek for, require.

res, rei, *f.*, thing, affair, circumstance ; practice (38) ; situation (44) ; **re** (24), by their action ; **re** (96), by its merits.

reseco, -secui, -sectum (1), cut back.

resisto, -stiti, (3), resist.

respondeo, -di, -sum (2), answer, reply.

res publica, rei publicae, *f.*, the Republic, the state, commonwealth ; public affairs (64).

restricte, *adv.*, narrowly, meanly

retineo, -tinui, -tentum (2), retain, keep.

revoco (1), recall.

rex, regis, *m.*, king.

ritus, -us, *m.*, form, manner ; ritu pecudum, like beasts (32).

rogatio, -ionis, *f.*, asking.

rogatus, -us, *m.*, *only in abl. sing.*, asking, request.

rogo, (1), ask, ask for.

Romanus, -a, -um, Roman ; *as noun*, a Roman.

rursus, *adv.*, again, back.

rusticatio, -ionis, *f.*, holiday in the country.

sacerdotium, -i, *n.*, priestly office.

saeculum, -i, *n.*, age.

saepe, *adv.*, often ; *compar.* saepius, too often.

sal, salis, *m.*, salt.

salus, -utis, *f.*, safety, salvation.

sancio, -nxi, -nctum (4), ratify, establish.

sanctus, -a, -um, pure (39), holy.

sane, *adv.*, certainly, by all means.

sapiens, -ntis, wise ; *as noun*, a philosopher.

sapientia, -ae, *f.*, wisdom, philosophy.

sat, satis, *adv.*, enough, sufficiently.

satietas, -tatis, *f.*, satiety, surfeit.

saxum, -i, *n.*, stone.

scelus, -eris, *n.*, crime, wickedness.

scena, -ae, *f.*, stage.

scio (4), know ; **haud scio an,** I rather think.

scitus, -a, -um, knowing, clever, shrewd.

scribo, scripsi, scriptum (3), write.

se, (sese), **sui, sibi, se,** *reflexive pronoun*, himself, herself, itself ; themselves.

secerno, -crevi, -cretum (3), separate, distinguish.

secundus, -a, -um, second ; prosperous ; **res prosperae,** prosperity.

securitas, -tatis, *f.*, freedom from care.

secus, *adv.*, differently, otherwise.

sed, *conj.*, but.

sedeo, sedi, sessum (2), sit.

semel, *adv.*, once.

semper, *adv.*, always.

sempiternus, -a, -um, everlasting.

senatus, -us, *m.*, the senate.

senectus, -tutis, *f.*, old age.

senex, senis (*compar.*, senior), old, aged ; *as noun*, old man.

sensus, -us, *m.*, sensation (14) ; feeling (27, 32) ; sentiment (92) ; pain (12).

sententia, -ae, *f.,* opinion ; main point (3) ; view (56).

sentio, sensi, sensum (4), feel, perceive ; realise (84).

septem, seven.

sequor, secutus (3), follow.

sermo, -onis, *m.,* speech, conversation, dissertation, discourse.

sero, *adv.,* too late.

serpo, -psi, -ptum (3), creep, spread gradually.

serus, -a, -um, late, too late.

servio (4), +*dat.,* be a slave to.

servitus, -tutis, *f.,* slavery, servitude.

servo (1), preserve, keep.

seu (sive), *conj.,* or if ; **seu ... seu,** whether . . . or.

severitas, -tatis, *f.,* seriousness.

severus, -a, -um, serious.

si, *conj.,* if.

sic, *adv.,* thus, so, in such a way.

sicut, *adv.,* just as, as.

sidus, -eris, *n.,* constellation, star.

significatio, -ionis, *f.,* evidence, indication.

signum, -i, *n.,* sign, mark.

silvestris, -e, wooded.

similis, -e, *with gen. or dat.,* like, similar ; kindred (26, 48).

similitudo, -inis, *f.,* likeness (50), similarity (81), comparison.

simplex, -icis, frank, open.

simul, *adv.,* at the same time, together.

simulatio, -ionis, *f.,* pretence.

simulo (1), pretend, counterfeit.

sin, but if.

sincerus, -a, -um, sincere, genuine.

sine, *prep. with abl.,* without.

singuli, -ae, -a, one each.

sino, sivi, situm (3), allow.

siquidem, *conj.,* if indeed.

sive, *see* **seu.**

socer, -eri, *m.,* father-in-law.

societas, -tatis, *f.,* union (83), association with (64), tie.

socius, -i, *m.,* ally ; comrade, companion.

sol, solis, *m.,* sun.

solacium, -i, *n.,* consolation.

soleo, solitus sum (2), *semi-dep.,* be accustomed, be wont.

solitarius, -a, -um, alone, solitary (88).

solitudo, -inis, *f.,* solitude.

sollicitus, -a, -um, anxious.

solum, *adv.,* only.

solus, -a, -um, alone.

sordidus, -a, -um, sordid, mean.

soror, -oris, *f.,* sister.

spatium, -i, *n.,* the right track.

species, -ei, *f.,* appearance.

spectatus, -a, -um, (proved), of established reputation (9).

specto (1), look at, examine.

sperno, sprevi, spretum (3), despise, spurn.

spero (1), hope, hope for.

spes, spei, *f.,* hope, expectation (11).

splendidus, -a, -um, splendid.

stabilis, -e, firm, stable, lasting.

stabilitas, -tatis, *f.,* firmness ; permanence (100).

statim, *adv.,* immediately.

statuo, -ui, -utum (3), settle, determine ; enact (42).

stirps, stirpis, *f.,* race, lineage.

sto, steti, statum (1), stand, stand up (24).

studeo (2), be eager, take pains.
studiose, *adv.*, eagerly.
studiosus, -a, -um, eager, keen on.
studium, -i, *n.*, eagerness, desire (26), zeal (44) ; pursuit (15, 74) ; devotion to study (71) ; affection (29, 49) ; *in pl.*, tastes (74, 77).
stultus, -a, -um, foolish.
suadeo, **suasi**, **suasum** (2), advise, persuade.
suavis, -e, pleasant.
suavitas, -tatis, *f.*, affability.
sub, *prep. with acc. and abl.*, under ; *of time*, towards, just before.
subdifficilis, -e, somewhat difficult.
subeo, -ire, -ii, -itum, undergo, risk.
subito, *adv.*, suddenly.
sublevo (1), sustain.
submitto, -misi, -missum (3), lower.
subterfugio, -ere, -fugi, escape.
subtiliter (*comp.* subtilius), finely, critically.
suffragium, -i, *n.*, vote.
sum, **esse**, **fui**, be, exist.
summus, -a, -um, highest, most excellent ; fullest (15), utmost (25).
sumo, **sumpsi**, **sumptum** (3), take (38), don (1).
supellex, -ectilis, *f.*, furniture.
super, *prep. with acc. and abl.*, above, beyond ; *as adv.*, over.
superbia, -ae, pride, arrogance.
superbus, -a, -um, proud, arrogant.
superior, -ius, higher superior ; former (20).

supero (1), surpass.
superus, -a, -um, high, above.
suppedito (1), supply.
supplicium, -i, *n.*, punishment.
supplico (1), entreat.
supra, *adv.*, above.
suscipio, -ere, -cepi, -ceptum, undertake ; incur (48, 77).
suspectus, -a, -um, suspected.
suspicio, -ere, -spexi, -spectum, look up to, admire.
suspicio, -ionis, *f.*, suspicion.
suspiciosus, -a, -um, suspicious.
suspicor (1), suspect.
sustineo, -ui, -tentum (2), endure, put up with ; check (63).
suus, -a, -um, his *or* her, *or* their own ; **sui**, -orum, friends (11, 70).

tabella, -ae, *f.*, ballot.
talis, -e, of such a kind, such.
tam, *adv.*, so.
tamen, *adv.*, however, nevertheless.
tamquam, *adv.*, as though, as it were.
tandem, *adv.*, at length, at last.
tantum, *adv.*, so much ; only (17).
tantus, -a, -um, so great, so much.
Tarentinus, -a, -um, of Tarentum (town in S. Italy).
tego, **texi**, **tectum** (3), protect.
telum, -i, *n.*, weapon.
temeritas, -tatis, *f.*, rashness ; fickle behaviour (20).
temperantia, -ae, *f.*, temperance, self-control.
tempto (1), try, test.

tempus, -oris, *n.*, time.

teneo, -ui, tentum (2), hold, hold fast to, keep.

tener, -era, -erum, tender (48) ; young (67).

tenuis, -e, poor, meagre (86).

Terentianus, -a, -um, of Terence (*See* Vocabulary of Proper Names).

terminus, -i, *m.*, boundary line.

terra, -ae, *f.*, earth, ground.

tertius, -a, -um, third.

testimonium, -i, *n.*, evidence.

toga, -ae, *f.*, toga.

tolerabilis, -e, tolerable, endurable.

tollo, sustuli, sublatum (3), remove, destroy; eliminate (19).

tortuosus, -a, -um, tortuous.

tot, *indecl.*, so many.

totus, -a, -um, whole, entire.

tractabilis, -e, pliant, elastic.

tracto (1), discuss.

trado, -didi, -ditum (3), hand over, give up.

traho, traxi, tractum (3), draw, drag.

tranquillitas, -tatis, *f.*, tranquillity, peace.

transfero, -ferre, -tuli, -latum, transfer.

tres, tria, *gen.* trium, *dat. and abl.* tribus, three.

tribunatus, -us, *m.*, tribuneship.

tribunus, -i, *m.*, tribune.

tribuo, -ui, -utum (3), bestow upon (9, 103) ; pay (13, 78) ; give (6).

triduum, -i, *n.*, three days.

tristitia, -ae, *f.*, melancholy, gloominess.

Troia, -ae, *f.*, Troy.

truncus, -i, *m.*, trunk.

tu, te, *etc.*, you (*sing.*).

tueor (2), protect.

tum, *adv.*, then, at that time ; further ; tum . . . tum, at one time . . . at another.

tunc, *adv.*, at that time.

turpis, -e, base, disgraceful.

turpitudo, -inis, *f.*, disgrace.

tuus, -a, -um, your (*sing.*) ; tui, -orum, your friends.

tyrannus, -i, *m.*, tyrant.

ubi, *adv.*, where, when, how (51).

ullus, -a, -um, any.

ultro, *adv.*, beyond, actually.

una, *adv.*, together.

universus, -a, -um, whole, entire.

unquam, *adv.*, ever.

unus, -a, -um, one ; alone ; ad unum, to a man (86).

urbs, urbis, *f.*, city.

uspiam, *adv.*, somewhere.

usque, *adv.*, right on ; usque ad (33), right up to.

usurpo (1), perform (8) ; cherish, dwell on (28).

usus, -us, *m.*, use, intercourse (29) ; experience (6, 18) ; friendship, intimacy (32, 76, 85) ; practice (52).

ut, *conj.*, as, since, when ; *with subj.*, in order that, that.

uter, -tra, -trum, which (of two)?

uterque, -traque, -trumque, each (of two), both ; utraque in re (64), in both events.

utilitas, -tatis, *f.*, usefulness (88), advantage (26, 51, 86, 100) ; interests (75).

utor, usus (3), +*abl.*, use, employ ; adopt (61).

utrum, *adv.*, whether, if.

uxorius, -a, -um, matrimonial.

vaco (1), be free from.

valeo (2), be strong (23, 68) ; be in good health (8) ; prevail (97) ; have weight (13, 99) ; have meaning (92) ; plurimum valere (44), have most weight ; valere ad (66), have the effect of.

valetudo, -inis, *f.*, health (20) ; ill-health (8).

vanitas, -tatis, *f.*, emptiness (99) ; insincerity (94).

vanus, -a, -um, empty, vain.

varius, -a, -um, various, varied.

vas, vasis, *n.*, vessel ; *pl.*, vasa, plate.

vaticinor (1), sing in inspired verse.

-ve, *enclitic conj.*, or.

vehementer, *adv.*, vehemently.

vel, *conj.*, or ; vel . . . vel, either . . . or ; *as adv.*, even.

vendibilis, -e, plausible, popular.

venditatio, -ionis, *f.*, boasting.

venenum, -i, *n.*, poison.

venia, -ae, *f.*, indulgence.

venio, veni, ventum (4), come.

venor (1), hunt.

verbum, -i, *n.*, word.

vere, *adv.*, truly, with truth.

verecundia, -ae, *f.*, respect.

vereor (2), fear, respect.

veritas, -tatis, *f.*, truthfulness, sincerity (89) ; the truth (90, 97, etc.).

vero, *adv.*, truly, indeed ; however.

verso (1), treat contemptuously (99) ; *in pass.*, exist (102), be engaged in (64).

verto, -ti, -sum (3), turn.

verum, *conj.*, but.

verum, -i, *n.*, the truth.

verus, -a, -um, true, **real,** genuine.

vesper, -eri *or* -eris, *m.*, evening ; ad vesperum, at evening.

vester, -tra, -trum, your, yours (*2nd pers. plural*).

vestis, -is, *f.*, clothing, clothes.

vestitus, -us, *m.*, clothing.

veto, -ui, -itum (1), forbid.

vetulus, -a, -um, old, worn out.

vetus, -eris, old, of long standing ; *superl.*, veterrimus (67).

vetustas, -tatis, *f.*, old age, age.

vexo (1), vex, harass, disturb.

via, -ae, *f.*, way ; path (61).

vicissim, *adv.*, in turn, mutually.

vicissitudo, -inis, *f.*, interchange.

victus, -us, *m.*, food ; fare (86, 103).

video, vidi, visum (2), see ; *in pass.*, seem.

vigeo (2), be vigorous, be displayed (51).

viginti, twenty.

vinco, vici, victum (3), conquer, defeat, overcome.

vinculum, -i, *n.*, fetter.

vindico (1), punish, visit with punishment.

vinum, -i, *n.*, wine.

violo (1), do wrong.

vir, viri, *m.*, man ; **optimi viri** (33), gentlemen.

viridis, -e, green.

viriditas, -tatis, *f.,* freshness.

virilis, -e, manly.

virtus, -tutis, *f.,* virtue ; merit (11).

virus, -i, *n.,* poison, venom.

vis, vim, *abl.* **vi,** *f.,* force, power, essence (15) ; *in plur.,* **vires, -ium,** strength.

visum, -i, *n.,* vision.

vita, -ae, *f.,* life.

vitalis, -e, vital ; **vita vitalis** (22), real life.

vitiosus, -a, -um, faulty, vicious.

vitium, -i, *n.,* vice, fault (78) ; harm (38).

vitupero (1), blame.

vivo, -xi, -ctum (3), live, spend one's life (15).

vivum, -i, *n.,* the quick.

vix, *adv.,* scarcely, hardly.

voco (1), call.

volo, velle, volui, wish, **be** willing.

volucer, -cris, -cre, winged, in the air (80).

voluntarius, -a, -um, voluntary, spontaneous.

voluntas, -tatis, *f.,* wish (61, 92) ; aim (15), inclination (61) ; feeling (58).

voluptas, -tatis, *f.,* pleasure ; physical pleasure.

vos, you (*pl.*).

vox, vocis, *f.,* voice, saying (37, 59).

vulgaris, -e, common, ordinary.

vulgus, -i, *n.,* common *or* ordinary people.

vultus, -us, *m.,* expression, look.

VOCABULARY OF PROPER NAMES

Aemilius Papus (2), *m.*, friend of Gaius Luscinus and his colleague in the consulship (282, 278 B.C.) and in the censorship (275 B.C.).

Africanus, -i, *m.*, see Scipio.

Agrigentinus, -a, -um, of Agrigentum. Vir Agrigentinus is Empedocles, the famous Greek philosopher *c.* 444 B.C.

Andria, -ae, *f.*, the ' Andrian Girl,' the title of a play of Terence.

Apollo, -inis, *m.*, the Greek god (Apollo), known also as Phoebus. He possessed many powers, including that of prophecy, which he exercised especially through the oracle at Delphi.

Archytas, -ae, *m.*, a philosopher and mathematician of the Pythagorean school, and a native of Tarentum (South Italy). He flourished about the year 400 B.C.

Athenae, -arum, *f. pl.*, Athens.

Atilius, -i, *m.*, Lucius Atilius, a Roman jurist (*c.* 150 B.C.) whose knowledge of civil law won him the title of Sapiens (6).

Atticus, -i, *m.* (109-32 B.C.), a very close friend of Cicero to whom his essay the De Amicitia was dedicated. The two men corresponded frequently and many of Cicero's letters to Atticus have been preserved.

Bias, Biantis, *m.*, one of the ' Seven Wise Men ' of Greece, and a native of Priene in Asia Minor. He flourished about 550 B.C. See the note on Chap. XVI., l. 42.

Blossius, -i, *m.*, Gaius Blossius, an ardent supporter of Tiberius Gracchus. See Chap. XI., Section 37.

Brutus, -i, *m.*, Decimus Junius Brutus, a member of the governing class in Rome, and consul in 138 B.C. The following year he subdued a part of Lusitania (Portugal). At the time of this dialogue, 129 B.C., he was an augur (7).

Capitolium, -i, *n.*, the Capitol, the temple of Jupiter Maximus Optimus, situated on the S.W. summit of the Capitoline Hill in Rome.

Carbo, -onis, *m.*, Gaius Papirius Carbo (164-119 B.C.) was a keen supporter of Tiberius Gracchus. See the note on Chap. XII., l. 15, l. 19, and Chap. XXV., l. 36.

Cassius, -i, *m.*, Spurius Cassius Vecellinus, a patrician of the early fifth century B.C., who, after a distinguished record of public service was accused by his fellow-patricians of aiming at the kingship, and put to death. See the note on Chap. XI, l. 5.

Cato, -onis, *m.* (39), Gaius Porcius Cato, a member of one of the ruling families in Rome and a follower of Tiberius Gracchus.

Cato, -onis, *m.*, Marcus Porcius Cato (234–149 B.C.), distinguished for his military ability, integrity, and unbending severity. See the note on Chap. I., l. 36. Cicero used him as the mouthpiece for his essay on 'Old Age'.

Coriolanus, -i, *m.*, Gaius Marcius Coriolanus. See the note on Chap. XI., l. 3.

Coruncanius, -i, *m.*, Titus Coruncanius, consul in 280 B.C. and famed for his knowledge of law in which he was the first to give public instruction at Rome.

Crassus, -i, *m.*, Gaius Licinius Crassus, author of the proposed reform for the manner of filling up vacancies in the Colleges of the Pontifices. Tribune of the Plebs in 145 B.C.

Curius, -i, *m.*, Manius Curius Dentatus, one of the heroes of Roman History (early third century B.C.), was famous in later times as an example of public service, frugality and virtue.

Ennius, -i, *m.*, Quintus Ennius (239–169 B.C.), the greatest figure among the early Roman poets. See the note on Chap. VI., l. 23.

Epiclerus, -i, *m.*, the Epiclerus or 'Heiress', the title of a play of Menander.

Fabricius, -i, *m.*, Gaius Fabricius Luscinus, one of the heroes of Roman History, and a contemporary of Curius with whom his name is often linked ; he was famous in later times as an example of public service, frugality, virtue and honour.

Fannius, -i, *m.*, Gaius Fannius Strabo, son-in-law of Laelius and one of the speakers in this essay 'On Friendship'.

Furius, -i, *m.*, Lucius Furius Philus, a member of the Scipionic circle and a friend of Laelius.

Gallus, -i, *m.*, Gaius Sulpicius Gallus, consul in 166 B.C., and an accomplished orator and man of culture.

Gnatho, -onis, *m.,* Gnatho, a character in Terence's play, 'the Eunuchus '.

Gracchus, -i, *m.* (1), Tiberius Sempronius Gracchus (167–132 B.C.), a member of a distinguished Roman family and famous for his attempts at reform during his tribunate 133 B.C. See the Introduction.

Gracchus, -i, *m.* (2), Gaius Sempronius Gracchus, brother of the above, and an equally ardent reformer. Tribune in 123–122 and 122–121 B.C. See the Introduction and the note on Chap. XI., l. 48.

Gracchus, -i, *m.* (3), Section 101. Tiberius Sempronius Gracchus, father of the Gracchi brothers and father-in-law of Scipio Africanus the younger.

Hannibal, -alis, *m.,* Hannibal, the famous Carthaginian general (247–183 B.C.) and sworn enemy of the Romans.

Laelius, -i, *m.,* Gaius Laelius, surnamed Sapiens and intimate friend of Scipio Africanus the younger. He is the chief speaker in this dialogue, ' On Friendship '. See the note on Chap. I., l. 1.

Laenas, -atis, *m.,* Publius Papilius Laenas, consul in 132 B.C. He was a member of the committee appointed to prosecute the followers of Tiberius Gracchus.

Latini, -orum, *m.,* Latins. See the note on Chap. III., l. 40.

Luscinus, -i, *m., see* Fabricius.

Lycomedes, -is, *m.,* Lycomedes, king of the Dolopians in Scyros and grandfather of Neoptolemus.

Maelius, -i, *m.,* Spurius Maelius, a rich plebeian who incurred the suspicions of the patricians by distributing corn to the poor of Rome during a great famine in B.C. 440–439. He was accused of aiming at royal power and subsequently slain. See the note on Chap. XI., l. 5.

Mancinus, -i, *m.,* Lucius Hostilius Mancinus, consul in 145 B.C. with Quintus Maximus.

Manilius, -i, *m.,* Manius Manilius Nepos, consul in 149 B.C., and famous as a jurist.

Maximus, -i, *m.,* Quintus Fabius Maximus Aemilianus, an elder brother of Scipio Africanus the younger ; consul in 145 B.C.

Metellus, -i, *m.,* Quintus Caecilius Metellus, a fellow augur of Laelius and estranged from Scipio by reason of political differences.

Minerva, -ae, *f.,* the goddess Minerva.

Mucius, -i, *m.,* Quintus Mucius Scaevola, son-in-law of Laelius. See the note on Chap. I., l. 1.

Mummius, -i, *m.* (Section 69), Lucius Mummius, surnamed Achaicus for his victory over the Achaean League and the capture and sack of Corinth (146 B.C.).

Mummius, -i, *m.* (Section 101), Spurius Mummius, brother of the above and a close friend of Scipio Africanus the younger and Laelius.

Nasica, -ae, *m.,* Publius Cornelius Scipio Nasica Serapio, a member of the Scipio family who became so notorious for the part he played in the murder of Tiberius Gracchus that he had to leave Italy.

Neoptolemus, -i, *m.,* son of Achilles by a daughter of Lycomedes. Because it had been prophesied that Troy would be captured only by the aid of Neoptolemus and Philoctetes, he was fetched by Ulysses from his grandfather's home in Scyros and, along with Philoctetes, sailed for Troy. He is also known as Pyrrhus.

Orestes, -is, *m.,* son of Agamemnon and Clytemnestra. The incident referred to in the text is explained in the note on Chap. VII., l. 29.

Pacuvius, -i, *m.,* Marcus Pacuvius (220–132 B.C.), a nephew of Ennius and the translator of many Greek tragedies for the Roman stage.

Papirius, *see* Carbo.

Paulus, -i, *m.,* Lucius Aemilius Paulus, successful Roman general. Two of his sons were adopted into other families, one being Scipio Africanus the younger. In Section 9 Laelius refers to the fortitude with which he bore the loss of his two younger sons who died within a week of each other.

Philus, -i, *m.,* Lucius Furius Philus, a member of the Scipionic circle and a friend of Laelius.

Pompeius, -i, *m.* (Section 77), Quintus Pompeius, consul in 141 B.C. Scipio quarrelled with him on Laelius' account (*see* Chap. XXI., l. 21).

Pompeius, -i, *m.* (Section 2).   Quintus Pompeius Rufus, consul in 88 B.C., a zealous supporter of the governing class.

Pylades, -is, *m.,* Pylades, the faithful friend of Orestes (*see* Section 24).

Pyrrhus, -i, *m.,* Pyrrhus, king of Epirus (modern Albania) 318–272 B.C.   See the note on Chap. VIII., l. 42.

Rupilius, -i, *m.* (1), Publius Rupilius, consul in 132 B.C. and a member of the commission appointed to examine the followers of Tiberius Gracchus.

Rupilius, -i, *m.* (2), Lucius Rupilius, a younger brother of the above.

Rutilius, -i, *m.,* Publius Rutilius, a young man in whose company Laelius found pleasure.

Scaevola, -ae, *m.,* the name of a family of the Mucian gens which included Quintus Mucius Scaevola the augur (*see* Mucius), and Quintus Mucius Scaevola the pontifex maximus, for whom see the note on Chap. I., l. 10.

Scipio, -ionis, *m.,* a son of Lucius Aemilius Paulus who was adopted into the Scipio family by the elder son of Publius Cornelius Scipio Africanus Major ('the elder'), the conqueror of Hannibal.   His full names (Publius Cornelius Scipio Aemilianus Africanus Minor) illustrate his career.   The first three are the names of his adoptive father ; Aemilianus is obtained from the fact that his real father's sister Aemilia was the wife of Africanus the elder ; Africanus is the title bestowed on him for his capture of Carthage in 146 B.C., while Minor is to distinguish him from Africanus Major.   In addition to a brilliant career in the service of his country, he was famous for his friendship with Laelius and his devotion to literature and culture.   In this way he became the centre of a literary set, often called the Scipionic circle.   See also the notes on Chap. I., l. 26, and Chap. XII., l. 13.   His dates are 185–129 B.C.

Sulpicius, -i, *m.,* Publius Sulpicius Rufus, tribune of the plebs in 88 B.C.   Previously a supporter of the governing class and a friend of Pompeius Rufus, in 88 B.C. he threw in his lot with the popular party and so quarrelled with his former friend Pompeius Rufus who happened to be consul at the time.

Tarquinius, -i, *m.,* Tarquinius Superbus, the last of the seven kings of Rome whose cruelty and tyranny brought about his expulsion and the creation of the Roman Republic.

Terentianus, -a, -um, of Terentius, -i, *m.* Terence, the writer of comedies, born at Carthage in 195 B.C., came as a slave to Rome, and assumed the name of his master who had given him the best education of the day and later on his freedom. The success of his first play ' the Andria ' introduced him to the Scipionic circle, and Laelius and Scipio are both said to have assisted him in the composition of his plays all of which are based on Greek models. He died abroad in his thirty-fifth year, leaving behind him six plays.

Themistocles, -is, *m.,* Themistocles, one of the most famous of Athenian generals and statesmen. See the notes on Chap. XII., l. 34 and l. 39.

Timon, -onis, *m.,* an Athenian who lived towards the end of the fifth century B.C. Because he avoided the society of his fellow-men, he soon became a proverbial character for moroseness and misanthropy. He is the subject of one of Shakespeare's plays, ' Timon of Athens '.

Tubero, -onis, *m.,* Quintus Aelius Tubero, a member of the governing class, fierce opponent of the Gracchi brothers and a friend of Laelius.

Vecellinus, -i, *m., see* Cassius.

Verginius, -i, *m.,* Aulus Verginius.